DON'T BET AGAINST ME!

TYNDALE HOUSE PUBLISHERS, INC.
Carol Stream, Illinois

DEANNA FAVRE

FAVRE

WITH ANGELA HUNT

Don't bet against me!

beating the odds against breast cancer and in life

Visit Tyndale's exciting Web site at www.tyndale.com

TYNDALE and Tyndale's quill logo are registered trademarks of Tyndale House Publishers, Inc.

Don't Bet Against Me!: Beating the Odds Against Breast Cancer and in Life

Designed by Jennifer Ghionzoli

Edited by Dave Lindstedt

Library of Congress Cataloging-in-Publication Data

Favre, Deanna.
 Don't bet against me! : beating the odds against breast cancer and in life / Deanna Favre ; with Angela Hunt.
  p. cm.
 Includes bibliographical references.
  ISBN-13: 978-1-4143-1907-0 (hc : alk. paper)
  ISBN-10: 1-4143-1907-X (hc : alk. paper)
  ISBN-13: 978-1-4143-1908-7 (sc : alk. paper)
  ISBN-10: 1-4143-1908-8 (sc : alk. paper)
  1. Favre, Deanna—Health. 2. Breast—Cancer—Patients—United States—Biography.
3. Football players' spouses—Biography.—I. Hunt, Angela Elwell, date. II. Title.
RC280.B8F38 2007
362.196'994490092—dc22
[B]   2007027978

Printed in the United States of America.

16 15 14 13 12 11 10 09 08
11 10 9 8 7 6 5 4 3 2 1

Brett ~ You inspire me. I have watched you deal with so much adversity, yet you never back down. You always face things head on. I gain a lot of strength from you just by seeing how you deal with your own adversity. You are definitely one of the strongest people I know. I feel very blessed to have you in my life. I have always been in love with you and I always will be.

Britt ~ We've gone through so much together. I will always admire you for who you became with all the obstacles you had to face. I am amazed daily by your intelligence, strength, persistence, and beauty. I am so proud of the person you have become. I am so blessed that you are in my life, and I love you very much.

Bre ~ Your smile is contagious. Your dramatic ways have brought so much laughter to our lives. You are so fun-loving—no doubt something you inherited from your dad. Your compassion for others is like none I have ever seen in a child of your age. Thanks for always taking my side. You are a blessing. I love you.

Mom ~ You are an amazing and remarkable woman. I would not be the person I am today were it not for you. You taught me to be humble, compassionate, loving, and generous. I will always be grateful that God gave me you as my mom. You give new meaning to the words *unconditional love*. I will always be grateful for you. I love you.

Dad ~ Thanks so much for all your support over the years, and for taking such good care of our family. I appreciate the sacrifices you made for me.

Christie ~ My sister, my best friend, there were times when I could not have made it through without your support. I know what we have is real because it goes back a long, long way. I never question our bond and the love and friendship we share. Our relationship means more to me than you will ever know. Thank you for your love and support through the years. You are one of the most intelligent and beautiful women I have ever known. You've made my life worthwhile. I can't imagine a single day without you. I love you dearly.

Josh ~ You are a wonderful brother-in-law. Thanks for sacrificing so much for my family. I cannot thank you enough for taking care of Brittany and treating her as you would your own child. What a gift you are to our family. I love you.

All the Favres ~ Thanks for so many wonderful memories over the years. These are memories I will treasure for a lifetime. I've been blessed to be a part of your family.

To my brother, Casey, and to Rocky Byrd and Irvin Favre— I love and miss you all dearly.

CONTENTS

ACKNOWLEDGMENTS

Thank you, Becca Duff, for helping me get my story on paper and inspiring me to tell it from the heart. You truly have a gift.

Thanks also to Angela Hunt, for all your help in shaping my story and bringing it to life.

Carol, thank you so much for coming to me with this wonderful opportunity. It has been such a pleasure working with and getting to know you. I look forward to our continued friendship in the future.

Thanks to all the wonderful people at Quad Graphics, for your continued efforts in serving the needs of people in your community and statewide. Wisconsin is lucky to have you!

Thanks to my team at the Van Dyke Haebler Center, Columbia St. Mary's, Memorial Sloan-Kettering, St. Vincent's Hospital in Green Bay, and The Cancer Center in Hattiesburg, MS. I appreciate your care and support more than you will ever know!

Thank you, Tim McGraw and the Dance Hall Doctors, and Faith Hill and her band, for being so selfless in your efforts to help those less fortunate through your work with the Favre Fourward Foundation and the HOPE Foundation.

Bus and Jeannine, thank you both so much for your continued friendship over the years. Bus, thank you for sharing your expertise, always looking out for us, and never complaining.

To all my friends in Mississippi and Wisconsin, thank you for always being there for me, and for your continued support.

And finally, to Packer fans, both in Green Bay and across the country, thank you all for your undying support. You are, and always will be, the greatest fans in the world!

For a man who prides himself on courage, toughness, and determination, I found out I only *thought* I knew what those words meant. When my wife was diagnosed with cancer, she showed me their true meaning. My father had passed away suddenly just ten months before, and Deanna's brother, Casey, passed away only a week before the cancer entered our lives. Deanna has always been a very strong, caring, thoughtful, and supportive person, and I can tell you that none of those qualities were lost during or after her fight.

I learned during all this that life is precious, sometimes short, and never easy, regardless of what people think. Money and fame cannot bring happiness. They cannot bring my dad or Casey back. My wife has always been a mountain among hills, and true to form she has turned her adversity into hope for other women in similar situations. Deanna often tells me I don't realize the impact or effect I have on people. Well, the feeling is mutual. I love her, and I would not be here today without her.

Brett Favre

Ask any cancer patient and they'll tell you about the nausea. The needle sticks. And the fear.

Especially the fear.

What they won't always tell you about is the waiting— what feels like days and weeks of interrupted life. They may not tell you about the unanchored feeling that creeps up like a burglar when the routine that has given shape and purpose to your days is suspended.

I've waited in doctors' offices, on exam tables, and by the telephone. Today I'm waiting at the hospital, drawn here by the necessity of surgery. Since my arrival, I've met technicians, nurses, and interns, all of whom greet me with a quick smile and study my chart without seeming to realize that the fate of my family depends on the notations on that page.

I'm wearing only a thin cotton gown, and the air conditioning is blowing full blast, probably to keep the surgical team cool as they prepare to operate.

"We're ready." A gowned nurse smiles at me from behind her mask. Her hands grip the bars on the side of the gurney, and for an instant her eyes meet my sister's. "You can wait in the reception area, ma'am. It's just outside, through those double doors and down the hall."

Christie squeezes my hand one more time, and I can't help clinging to the welcome warmth of her fingers. A shivering rises from someplace deep within me, and I lock my jaw to keep my teeth from chattering.

I always shiver when I'm nervous.

The nurse notices the gooseflesh on my arms. "I know it's cold," she says, a note of apology in her voice. "Sorry about that. But we'll have you under a blanket when you wake up."

Then I am rolling out of the room, speckled ceiling tiles sliding past my eyes. The nurse bumps a door with her hip; I hear the soft thud and a squeak as the doors open and we enter the operating theater.

My surgeon, Dr. Alexandria Heerdt, is waiting inside, and I'm relieved by the sight of her friendly smile. "How are you doing, Deanna?" she asks, her voice slightly muffled by her mask.

I'd like to answer, but I'm distracted by the nurse, who seems determined to jab a hole into the back of my left hand. She's trying to start an IV for the anesthetic, but few nurses have ever been able to find a vein on my left side.

"Try my right hand," I say, anxiety welling up in my throat. "For some reason the veins on my left—"

"We prefer the left," the nurse says, sticking me again. "That way we stay out of the doctor's way."

I zip my lip as the nurse sighs in exasperation. The tumor is near my right breast, so I suppose I understand, but these ineffective needle pricks are not helping me relax.

"Try the right hand," Dr. Heerdt says, her voice calm.

I close my eyes as the nurse stands and walks to the other side of the table. A moment later, I feel a prick in my right hand, and then the room grows blurry.

Gloved hands surround me. Hands open my gown and swab a cold liquid over my right breast and the skin beneath my arm. Every muscle in my body contracts in a shiver. I want to tell them I'm freezing, but my tongue won't move.

Hands lift my left arm and slip a blood-pressure cuff around my biceps. Other hands press electrocardiograph monitors to my chest and tape them in place. My fingertip feels a light pinch as hands position the clip that will measure my blood oxygen levels.

I try to look for my doctor, but my heavy eyelids have frozen shut. Somewhere in the darkness, hands have adjusted the IV that is pouring anesthetic into my body, numbing all sensation.

My skin contracts in another slow shiver. Why didn't they tell me I'd be so cold?

The surgeon will soon take her chilly scalpel and open my breast, removing the cancer that threatens my life.

Until then, I can do nothing but wait, sleep . . . and hope.

world champions

As Dan Aykroyd, John Goodman, and James Belushi gyrated through their halftime performance as the Blues Brothers, I grinned at my sister, breathed in the scent of hot dogs and popcorn, and resisted the urge to pinch myself. We were halfway through Super Bowl XXXI, Green Bay was leading New England 27–14, and I was *sure* we'd beat the Patriots . . . despite the fact that my husband had been sacked on the final play of the first half.

Brett and the team had worked hard to earn this trip to New Orleans. The Packers had just completed a phenomenal season, and their 13–3 record was the best in the NFC. Led by Reggie White, the "Minister of Defense," the Packer defense that season had allowed only 210 points while the offense, led by my husband, had scored an NFL-best 456 points. Seven times they had outscored their opponent by at least three touchdowns.

I took quiet pride in the Packers' accomplishments, because

Brett had won the NFL's Most Valuable Player award for the second straight year. During the season, he had thrown for 3,899 yards and thirty-nine touchdowns (at the time, an NFC record).

But as outstanding as his athletic victories were, I was even more proud of his personal accomplishments. In May 1996, I had stood with Brett and his coach, Mike Holmgren, as Brett told a crowd of reporters that he had developed an addiction to the painkiller Vicodin. Brett voluntarily entered the Menninger Clinic, a rehab center in Topeka, Kansas, where he remained for forty-six days. Now, eight months later, Brett looked and felt good. He and his teammates wanted to win the Super Bowl—and with all my heart, I believed they would.

As the halftime show ended and the teams ran back out onto the field, I told my brother and sister that I'd see them later. Because we weren't playing in our home stadium, we weren't sitting in a skybox—in fact, our tickets had been split, so I was sitting near the 20 yard line, with my friends Kristin and Dotsie, while my family and Brett's sat in other sections. And because New Orleans is only sixty miles from Kiln, our hometown in Mississippi, Brett had lots of other friends and family in the stadium as well.

I couldn't help but feel proud as I peered over the sea of heads and spotted Brett on the field. After going public with news of his addiction, he had lost a couple of endorsement deals, but I felt he was more of a role model now than before. He could have kept his addiction quiet and no one would have known—in fact, most people had trouble believing that an MVP who played as well as Brett did could have any kind of drug problem.

But Brett had told the world about his addiction, and then he'd done what he had to do to confront it. I knew that his public stance took a special kind of courage, one that doesn't come naturally to me.

I've always been a behind-the-scenes sort of person, and Super Bowl week had been a challenge. We'd traveled to New Orleans a full seven days before the game, and I'd spent most of that time avoiding the official events while I sought out kid-friendly activities for our soon-to-be-eight-year-old daughter, Brittany. It's not that I'm antisocial—it's just that I'm shy; and amid all the hype, the crowds, and the media frenzy of the Super Bowl, I felt like a fish out of water.

Because the quarterback is the most visible player on a team, and I was the quarterback's wife, I had been asked to appear on the TV show *Extra*. I agreed, and then wondered what in the world had possessed me to accept the invitation. It was one of the first times I had ever been formally interviewed, and it was one of the more uncomfortable experiences of my life. Brad Goode, the interviewer, was an honest-to-goodness celebrity, and I felt like a redneck country girl who'd stumbled into a formal ball.

To make matters worse, I'd come down with a bad case of strep throat while we were in New Orleans. The team doctors had diagnosed my illness and given me antibiotics, but I was still feeling as sick as a dog when Brad showed up with his camera crew. He thought he'd be interviewing me in a suite, but when he arrived and saw that Brittany, my two friends, and I had been crammed into a tiny hotel room, he decided that we should do the interview out in the hallway—like he'd just happened to bump into Brett Favre's wife in a New Orleans hotel.

So there we were, walking and chatting in a dimly lit hallway. I was struggling to remember not to look at the camera, while smiling and talking like I had a brain in my head. That's harder than it sounds, because I was completely intimidated by Brad Goode. He behaved like the professional interviewer he is and did his best to set me at ease. While I tried to smile and not trip over the trailing camera cords, Brad asked all the usual questions: "What's it like being married to Brett Favre?" "How do you feel about being at the Super Bowl?"

Well, I had no idea what to say. I had no idea how I felt about anything. I was sick and nervous and scared and felt like the most witless person in America. I said something and Brad looked at me like he was waiting for me to say more, but I didn't have a clue what he was expecting. I suppose his job is to encourage people to rattle on so they can get enough footage, and then someone can edit out the stupid stuff, but I kept thinking that if they edited out *my* stupid stuff, there'd be nothing left.

I'm sure I wasn't the most vivacious guest that Brad Goode has ever interviewed. He's lucky I didn't pass out on camera.

To this day, I've not seen that interview, and I could die happy without ever seeing it. For someone as shy as I am, answering questions on camera isn't easy. Brett and I are from a small town, so we're not what you'd call glittery people. We grew up in a rural area near the Gulf Coast, and we're far more comfortable in the country than under city lights. Brett may not feel at home in a tuxedo, but he's always felt perfectly at ease in a football stadium. As for me, I'd go anywhere to watch him play.

I'm always a little anxious when Brett's on the field. Professional football players don't hold anything back, and it only takes a split second for someone to be seriously injured. I hold my breath practically the entire game, praying that my husband will make it through four quarters without another concussion or any more broken bones.

After the second-half kickoff, the Packers pushed the

Patriots to their 37 yard line, but the drive stalled and New England took over on downs. After an exchange of punts, the Patriots drove fifty-three yards in seven plays and scored, cutting our lead to 27–21 with just under three and a half minutes to go in the third quarter. But on the following kickoff, the Packers' Desmond Howard returned the ball ninety-nine yards for a touchdown. Then Brett tossed a pass to tight end Mark Chmura for a two-point conversion, making the score 35–21, which proved to be the final margin of victory.[1]

TEN THINGS
every woman should know about football

1. In football, no one gets offended when men pat each other on the rear.

2. Dancing in the end zone is optional.

3. Packer fans love it when a player jumps into the stands after a touchdown. It's called the Lambeau Leap.

4. Helmet-butting is a sign of mutual respect.

5. When players gather in a huddle, they're calling plays, but they're also groaning about their aches and pains.

6. Favre rhymes with starve. Don't worry about the order of the letters.

7. That little fanny pack the quarterback wears is really a hand warmer—especially important in Green Bay.

8. It is perfectly acceptable to wear a block of cheese on your head at a Packer game.

9. When the players look like they're freezing to death out there on the field . . . they are.

10. Real men are not intimidated by pink Packer caps.

After Brett completed the two-point conversion, I glanced at a blue-and-silver–clad Patriots fan seated behind me and resisted the urge to gloat. Near the end of the first quarter, after Drew Bledsoe, the Pats' quarterback, had thrown a touchdown pass to give New England their only lead, this same fan had stood up and yelled, "Go back and get some Vicodin, Favre!"

I seethed as his words echoed over our section of the Superdome. Then I turned, looked the guy in the eye, and lifted my chin. "That's my husband," I told him, "and I'd appreciate it if we didn't go there today."

Startled, the man flushed and apologized, but not all fans are that civil . . . or that sober.

I'm older and wiser today, and I've learned that when you stand up and say anything to defend your team or a player, people usually don't apologize—they typically get louder and even more vicious. I was fortunate that day at the Super Bowl, because nobody else said anything nasty about Brett.

My first instinct is always to stand up and defend Brett, because he's my husband and my best friend. I think it's just human nature to do that sort of thing. But over the years I've learned that people are going to say negative things, and it's something I have to put up with—even if I don't want to grin and bear it. I've learned that those kinds of comments can't hurt me, and they don't hurt Brett. His play, his character, and his career speak for themselves, and I don't have to defend him.

But I'm not saying that rude comments can't make me uncomfortable. Two years after Super Bowl XXXI, Brittany and I were pelted with ice and cookies by 49er fans in San Francisco after someone recognized us as Brett Favre's wife and daughter. In stadiums all over the country, I've heard grown men shout childish, vulgar comments about the oppos-

ing team *and* their own team—and after that game against
the 49ers, I vowed I would never again bring my children to
sit in the stands at one of Brett's games. They don't need to
be subjected to that kind of abuse and those kinds of vulgar
comments.

At the San Francisco game, I put my arms around Brittany
and told her to ignore the people who were harassing us—but
the language was so bad, we probably should have left. I've
been back to San Francisco since then, and I've had better
experiences—I don't mean to blame the city, because any
stadium experience can be bad or good; it depends entirely on
whether the people seated around you are decent people.

At Super Bowl XXXI, when Reggie White sacked Drew
Bledsoe for a third time, with less than two minutes to go
in the game, and the Packers went on to claim their victory,
I wasn't focused on the crowd around me. My husband, my
childhood sweetheart, had found his niche and had scrambled
to the top of the game he loved. Our daughter was healthy,
beautiful, and brilliant. We had a lovely home, and Brett had
conquered his addiction to Vicodin.

After the game, I shouldered my way through the crowd
and made it to Brett's side. There were so many reporters,
it was almost impossible to get to him, but I managed to
get close enough to give him a hug and a kiss and tell him
I was proud of him. He held Brittany for a few moments
while I stood and basked in the glow of his well-deserved
victory.

"We're champions today because we overcame a lot of
adversity," Brett told a group of reporters during the postgame media crush. "Winning the Super Bowl so close to
home makes it extra special because I had so much family and
friends in the stadium watching."[2]

We were on top of the world.

Married to Mr. MVP

The next season, Brett's sixth with the Packers, passed in a wonderful and busy blur. Brett signed a seven-year contract extension and became the first NFL player to win the MVP award three times. He and the Packers battled through the playoffs and again earned a spot in the Super Bowl, this time in San Diego.

Brett had enjoyed another great season, leading the league with thirty-five passing touchdowns. The defensive line, again led by Reggie White, was an awesome force. The Packers went into the Super Bowl as odds-on favorites, especially considering they were the defending champions and the Broncos had made the playoffs as a wild-card team.

More than ninety million fans watched the game on television, a larger audience than any previous Super Bowl. I knew Brett was pumped up about the game, and he started well, completing three of his first four passes on the opening drive, including a twenty-two-yard touchdown pass to Antonio Freeman. But the Broncos answered with a touchdown of their own, and by halftime they held a 17–14 lead.

The second half opened with a fumble on the Broncos' first play from scrimmage, giving us the ball at the Denver 26, but after a couple of penalties hampered the drive, we ended up settling for a field goal to tie the score.

Denver took the lead again with a touchdown near the end of the third quarter, and the Packers fumbled the following kickoff and lost the ball. But then Eugene Robinson intercepted a John Elway pass in the end zone, and Brett led the team on an eighty-five-yard, four-play drive that tied the score again with thirteen and a half minutes to go in the game.

The teams traded punts for most of the fourth quarter, but just before the two-minute warning, the Broncos completed a pass that put the ball at the Packers' 8 yard line. After a hold-ing penalty set them back ten yards, the Broncos ran the ball down to the 1 yard line with 1:47 left in the game.

Hoping to conserve time on the clock to increase the team's chances for a potential game-tying drive in the final seconds, coach Mike Holmgren told the Packers to let the Broncos score on the next play, bringing the score to 31–24.

On the Packers' final drive, Brett completed four con-secutive passes, moving the ball to the Denver 31, but his next three passes were incomplete, and the ball went back to the Broncos on downs. John Elway took a knee on the final play of the game, and the Broncos had their first-ever Super Bowl victory.

We were discouraged—it's hard not to be after such a big game—but we were happy for John Elway, the Broncos' quarterback. He was nearing the end of his career and hadn't yet won a Super Bowl, and we have a lot of respect for him.

Most of the Packers went to the big postgame party, but Brett and I didn't feel the need to celebrate the loss. Instead, he and I took Brittany, my sister, Christie, and her husband, Josh, to a little restaurant where we could sit and simply enjoy being together. At one point during the meal, Brett stopped eating and looked at me. "Thank God," he said. "Thank God I have you and Brittany."

For me, football has never been the most important thing. My world has always been centered on family.

At that moment, I knew that my husband had begun to realize that family was more important than football, and that we'd be there for him when he was finished with the game. He hadn't always felt that way.

He later told a reporter, "There was a time when I thought football was the most important. Football will be over at some point; the family goes on. When you lose someone, or when there are setbacks, it kind of puts it in perspective. You can lose a game . . . it's a tough loss, you're down, two weeks later you forget about it. . . . But when you lose a family member or something tragic happens, that stays with you forever. You never get over it. . . . Football is important, but not as important as you once thought it was."[3]

For me, football has never been the most important thing. My world has always been centered on family.

a great catch

I adore my husband. Thousands of Packer fans do, too, but I know him better than anyone else does. He is one of the most wonderful people—a guy who avoids conflict whenever possible and wants everyone to be happy. He is a loving father to our girls and always gives me a hug and a kiss when he comes home.

If you're in a bad mood, Brett's the type to come over and do his best to make you laugh. He's a family man, and he's never happier than when he's working around our home or curled up in the den watching a movie or playing a game with me and the girls.

I am so blessed to have him in my life. He's given me opportunities I never would have had if I hadn't met him. Words could never express the depth of appreciation and admiration I have for him.

One of my girlfriends and I are always saying that we have to stay friends because we know too much about the other to become enemies. Brett and I could say the same thing about our relationship. We've been through a lot together, and we've come way too far to drift apart now.

Small-town girl

Although many people refer to me as the "better half" of a famous quarterback, who loves the game of football, at heart I'm a small-town girl. I'm happiest when I'm at home, surrounded by my family and far away from the spotlight.

I grew up in a modest home, and my parents both worked extremely hard my whole life. As the oldest child, I spent a lot of time taking care of my younger brother and sister, Casey and Christie. As a kid, I was extremely shy and felt more comfortable on a ball field than in social situations.

I've been told that I first met Brett in catechism class when I was seven years old. The story could be true, because we're only ten months apart in age, and Kiln (the *n* is silent) was so small in those days that it didn't even have a stoplight. Our school had only about 1,200 students, and that included everyone in first through twelfth grades. Every Wednesday after school, all the kids who went to the Catholic church got on a bus and went to catechism class.

I remember Brett as a child because he had a distinct, blond cowlick on the right side of his head. That cowlick stood out to me; I thought it was cute. But I don't remember the first time I met him; in fact, I can't remember a time when I didn't know who he was.

Brett's parents, Irvin and Bonita Favre, taught at our school, so I knew who they were too. Irvin coached football and baseball, and Bonita taught special education students.

Brett and I may have known each other since grade school, but we first began to *notice* each other when I was a sophomore in high school. I guess you could say we bonded over our love of sports. I played softball and basketball, and Brett played football, baseball, and basketball.

Right before our Christmas break in 1983, our paths began to cross more than usual. One afternoon, I was watching a basketball game after school with two of my friends. At one point, I turned and noticed Brett sitting by himself in the bleachers above us. He was wearing a pair of big high-top tennis shoes, but they were open and untied. Even though he looked a little goofy, I still thought he was cute.

My girlfriends must have thought so, too, because they kept peeking at him and elbowing me, distracting me from the game. "Ask him," one friend kept whispering. "Go ask him why he's wearing his shoes that way."

I rolled my eyes. "If you want to know so bad, you ask him."

"Come on, go on over there. Ask him."

Realizing that I wasn't going to get any relief until I did what they said, I sighed and climbed up to the bench where Brett was sitting. "Hey," I said. "Why don't you tie your shoes?"

He looked at me and blinked. "I don't know."

"Oh." I slipped my hands into my pockets. "Okay, then."

I went back and reported his answer, then tried to focus on the game.

Who is that guy?

The next week, after basketball practice, I had a little "encounter" with Brett in the girls' locker room. First, I should explain something about the layout of the locker room. Coming in from the gym, it had a swinging door without a latch, which opened onto a long hallway lined with hooks, a bench, and some open shelves for storage. Off the hallway was the locker area, and past that were the showers and toilets.

Because the seniors had first dibs on the lockers, the underclassmen usually dressed out in the hallway. We'd hang our clothes on the hooks and sit on the bench to pull on our shoes. Whenever our coach needed to come in to talk to us, he'd push the door open, avert his eyes, and yell "knock, knock" real loud. We all knew to be dressed by the time he yelled.

On this particular afternoon, my friend and I were in the hallway getting dressed for practice. I had my shorts on and had just pulled on my shirt when the door slammed open. I looked up, expecting to see our coach, but it wasn't him—it was Brett. I don't know if he and his brothers were horsing around outside and he got slammed into the door or what, but there he was, looking as surprised to see me as I was to see him. He gasped, turned, and walked away in a hurry. I looked at my friend as if to say, "What is going on in that boy's head?"

When I stepped out into the gym, I saw Brett, his older brother Scott, and Coach Johnson sitting in the bleachers. I asked Brett why he had opened the door, but he didn't give me an answer.

The next day, I found myself playing two-on-two basketball with Brett and a couple of friends. That was when I really began to appreciate him. Brett is a good basketball player—he's mobile, he's great at handling the ball, and he has tricks. For example, while we were playing and I was guarding him, squatted down in a defensive position, he bounced the ball through my legs, caught it on the other side, and made a layup. I was livid, and my face must have been beet red because he'd caught me with a move like that, but I was also impressed.

The next time he had the ball, I was ready for his little tricks. I put up my hands, pressured him, and finally dove for the ball, feeling a flush of pleasure when I took it from him. Of course, once I had the ball again, I would have been dipped alive in boiling oil before I'd let him take it from me without a challenge.

The following Friday night, Brett's mother invited the boys' and girls' basketball teams to their house for Scott Favre's seventeenth birthday. My cousin Vanessa asked me to go with her, and we picked out a shirt to give Scott for a birthday present. Brett, Scott, and Coach Favre had gone to a football game to get Scott out of the house, so Vanessa and I went inside with Mrs. Favre and waited for the boys to come home.

When Brett finally walked into the house, he looked at me and I looked at him, but we didn't speak, not at first. I think he was startled to find himself in the middle of a surprise party. He ran back out the door and came in another way so that Scott could walk in and be surprised. But as Brett ran out, I thought, *Oh, my goodness. He lives here.*

As the party went on, people split off into their own little groups, so I went outside and started shooting baskets. I didn't know it at the time, but Brett stood at the window and watched me for a while before he worked up enough courage to come out and grab the ball.

We were both shy and embarrassed at that age, but basketball was something we had in common. We started off just shooting around, and then we played a little one-on-one. Before the night ended, we went for a ride with Vanessa, got lost, and ended up at the town cemetery. Vanessa wasn't the best driver at that age, and she couldn't figure out how to get out of there. We were all scared to death.

At one point, Brett's hand brushed against mine, and he jerked his hand back like my skin was made of poison ivy.

Later he did work up the courage to hold my hand for about five seconds.

When we finally got back to his house, I walked with him up to the door. It didn't feel like the right time for a kiss, and I was worried about what I should do if he did try to kiss me. Besides, Vanessa and my friends were waiting for me in the car. Brett asked if he could call me, and I said yes. Then he leaned in to kiss me.

Now, the perfect kiss requires one person's head to move one way while the other person's head moves in the other direction. Maybe Brett and I had spent too much time playing basketball and trying to anticipate each other's moves, because we moved our heads in unison—once, twice, three times—before we finally figured out that in the sport of kissing, at least, it pays to move in *opposite* directions.

Later that weekend, Brett called me, and I could hear his brothers whispering in the background, "Ask her, ask her." I played it cool until he said, "Will you go with me?"

Covering the phone, I barked a laugh. Then I got back on the line and demurely replied, "Yes."

So I had a boyfriend . . . and the thing we had in common was sports. Our "dates" were not what you'd call exciting— we played catch a lot. As we spent time together, we became good friends, and I think that's one reason we've managed to stay together. As the years passed, there were days when I wasn't sure our relationship would last, but I've always loved him.

Love grew between us as we talked on the phone every night, mostly sharing our hopes for the future. "You know, D," he'd say, "it's going to happen. I'm going to play college football."

"I know you will."

Then he'd tell me how he was going to be so good he'd play professional football someday.

Everything he dreamed, I dreamed along with him. He could have told me he was planning to stand in Hattiesburg and throw a football across the state line, and I would have believed him.

Brett was my first love, my only love. He'd say, "We're going to get married some day," and I'd agree. We even talked about what we'd name our children . . . but I seem to remember that we only mentioned boys' names.

Brett was my first love, my only love.

And God sent us two girls. Funny how things work out, isn't it?

None of my girlfriends had boyfriends like Brett. He brought me the most unusual gifts. One day he gave me a catcher's mask and mitt because he wanted me to catch for him while he practiced pitching. When his dad saw Brett hurling fastballs into my glove, he came running out of the house. "Boy," he yelled, "you can't throw that hard to a girl!"

"Why not?" Brett frowned and looked at his dad. "She's catchin' it."

I was, and my hand was on fire, but I wasn't about to tell him that.

Brett's family was close-knit, and I often went with them to parades, cookouts, and games, of course. When Brett wasn't with me, he was with his family.

When Brett and I went to my senior prom, his parents were "working" the prom as sponsors of the senior class. Before leaving for dinner, Brett and I went to have our prom pictures taken. After the pictures, we got in the car and drove to the restaurant where we met up with a few other couples for dinner. But when we got there, Brett couldn't find his wallet. We finally realized that he had set it on top of the car and driven away without realizing it.

So we went to the prom hungry. When everyone heard what happened, the teachers wanted to chip in and give us money to eat, but we didn't want to accept it. So after the prom, we went to Shoney's with Brett's parents and ate breakfast buffet style.

Not the most romantic prom date, maybe, but memorable.

Our dates often took a dramatic turn. One day, while we were swimming at Brett's house, he and Scott started telling me about how they liked to jump from the roof of the pool house into the pool—they said they did it all the time. The pool house was a flat-roofed, single-room structure that held a picnic table, a grill, and a refrigerated drink box.

I was curious, so I got out, climbed onto the roof, and peered over the edge. Brett and Scott followed me up there, then grabbed my hands and said there was only one way down. Next thing I knew, they were backing up to get a running start, and taking me off the roof with them.

I thought I was going to die. The pool wasn't that big— not much wider than the three of us linked together—and it had a long diving board in the center. When we flew from the rooftop, that diving board seemed to be zooming straight for my head.

We managed to jump over the shallow end, avoid the diving board, and land in deep water, but I'll never know how I survived growing up with those Favre boys.

A rose is a rose

I wouldn't want you to think that Brett's courtship of me was all rough-and-tumble games. We did go out for dinner and to movies, and Brett learned about bringing a girl flowers.

I remember a time while we were in college when we decided to break up. We had weathered a few ups and downs before, but this time I decided we would *stay* broken up. I loved Brett, but our relationship just wasn't going to work. I determined that I wasn't going to answer his calls, let him in the house, or go out with him again.

For an entire month I held firm. When he called, I didn't answer. When he showed up at my apartment, I hid behind the curtains and left the lights off so he would think I wasn't home. I went out of my way to avoid him for four weeks, then five . . . and then one day he called, and I answered.

"I really don't like this," he said. "Do you want to go to a movie?"

Truth be told, I didn't like being apart, either, so I said yes.

When Brett came to pick me up, I opened the door and saw him standing on the porch with a single red rose in his hand. It was a plastic rose, mind you, but he'd never brought me a flower before. I was touched.

After a couple of days, he called and asked me to dinner. I agreed, because things were going pretty well between us, and this time he handed me a rose as we were getting in the car. Again, I was touched . . . and impressed. What had gotten into him?

A week later, he invited me out to dinner again, and I agreed. This time, as I got in the car, I saw a single red rose lying on the car seat. "Aw," I said. "How pretty."

As I picked up the flower, I read the little tag attached to the stem.

"Thank you," I said when he slid into his seat. "I guess this is the last one."

He shot me a quizzical look. "Why do you say that?"

I fingered the tag. "Because of what it says right here: three for ninety-nine cents."

He'd picked up those flowers at some bargain store and

decided to give them to me individually. A sweet idea, but he never gave me a single plastic rose again.

Unexpected detour

When I was a senior in high school, my parents moved to Poplarville, a town about forty miles north of Kiln, but I stayed behind so I could play basketball and possibly get a scholarship. Mom had always emphasized that we needed to go to college, so I had gathered up every ounce of my five-foot-six-inch self and aimed for a basketball scholarship . . . and got it.

After I graduated in 1986, I went to Pearl River Community College in Poplarville. One year later, when Brett graduated, he got the last available football scholarship at the University of Southern Mississippi—because someone else backed out. Brett was not one of those flashy high school quarterbacks who could have his pick of colleges—he was grateful for the chance to play at USM, because he actually *played* for four years, instead of being a backup or a redshirt at some other school. When he left for the NFL at age twenty-two, he had four full college seasons under his belt.

Although Brett signed at USM as a defensive back, one day the coach saw him throwing a football with some other guys and moved him to the number seven quarterback position. By the time the season started, he was number three. In hindsight, I can see how what appeared to be a lackluster beginning to his career was actually a blessing in disguise, because Brett was not subjected to the pressure that some young quarterbacks feel when moving up to the collegiate level.

Brett and I were still able to see each other in college, because our two schools were only about forty miles apart. I played basketball on scholarship, and I played softball, too.

Pearl River was an excellent place to take my basic college courses, and I looked forward to continuing my education at Southern Mississippi. But during the summer that I was preparing to transfer from junior college to the university, I discovered I was going to have a baby.

Suspecting I might be pregnant, I had visited a family planning center. But because I had experienced slight bleeding the month before, I didn't go in for the test until I had entered my second month. After the results came back positive, a social worker took me into her small office, sat me in a chair, and looked at me with a concerned expression. "What do you want to do?" she asked.

My insides tangled in a knot when I thought about how disappointed my mother and my grandparents would be when they heard the news. As hard as that was, I didn't even want to *think* about having an abortion. I knew I was carrying a baby. Though I hadn't planned to have a child at this point in my life (I was nineteen), there was no way I could destroy an innocent life.

"All I can do is have it," I told her. "So I will."

I'd be lying if I said I wasn't scared. I knew Brett would be upset, too, and at a time when he was trying to concentrate on school and football. He would probably wonder whether the baby would mean an end to his football career, and I was wondering how in the world I could feed a baby and myself, too.

On the way back to my apartment, I kept thinking of changes I would have to make. I had completed two years of college, but I needed two more years to earn a degree. I'd have to work part-time and go to school part-time—but I could do that; I'd held one job or another ever since I was old enough to fill out an application.

I wouldn't ask my parents for money, because I knew they didn't have it to give. They barely made ends meet themselves.

I have always been very independent, and I've always felt I could take care of myself. I saw the pregnancy as my responsibility. I was pregnant, and I would deal with it, end of story. I wasn't looking for anyone to help me out.

When I gave Brett the news, he agreed with me about keeping the baby and assured me that everything would be okay. Abortion has always been unacceptable for both of us. Adoption is a good option for some people, but I wanted to raise my child. I decided I would do whatever I had to do to take care of my baby.

A couple of well-meaning friends came to visit me at my apartment. "Maybe having a child isn't the best thing for you right now," one of them said. "You're nineteen, the timing's bad, you're not finished with college, and you don't have any way to support yourself, much less a baby—"

"I'm not going to get married because I *have* to get married," I said. "And I'm not going to have an abortion. I made a bad choice, and for every choice there's a consequence. So I'm going to deal with the consequences, and I'm going to have this baby."

What followed was an almost unfairly easy pregnancy. I gained only sixteen pounds, and I was able to keep up with my running and exercising workout routine even into my seventh month. I stayed active and had a relatively easy birth experience. Unfortunately, after the delivery, I began to hemorrhage and had to be given two units of blood. Thankfully, my mother, who had stayed with me, realized that something was terribly wrong and insisted that the nurses call my doctor. He was furious when he found out how bad things had gotten. Had my mother not been there and acted when she did, I might have died. When I left the hospital, I actually weighed less than I had before I got pregnant.

But it was all worth it. Brittany Nicole was born on February 6, 1989, weighing 7 lbs., 2 oz. When I held her in my arms for the first time, I knew I'd made the right decision. Brett was with me, and one of the reasons I liked the name Brittany was that "Britt" sounded similar to *Brett*.

I have always known that children are a gift from God, but I never really thought about what that meant until I had a daughter.

I have always known that children are a gift from God, but I never really thought about what that meant until I had a daughter. Brittany is so special, and I've always been happy that I had her. I didn't go about starting a family in the best way, but at least I made the decision to have her.

I am blessed because Brittany is in my life. She is so beautiful and smart—she's brought a lot to my life and she's taught me so much. She has also helped me to grow up.

Brittany was always so smart as a little girl, and very mature—and scientific—for her age. She was always inquisitive and would ask me questions about outer space and the moon. "If we can go to the moon, why can't we go to Mars?" she'd want to know.

Because I had no idea how to explain it, I'd get books for her and say, "Maybe you can read about that and write a report on it." She loved that idea, so we'd get a book on the solar system and she'd read and tell me all about it. Later, I bought her a child's encyclopedia, and she loved doing research.

Once, however, when Britt was four or five, we met Brett's cousin Jan, who was pregnant. After looking at Jan's belly, Brittany asked me, "How is Jan going to get that baby out of her stomach?"

"Well," I said, "the doctor has some special tools, and he's going to help her get the baby out."

Britt considered this a moment, then looked at me again. "Well, how'd she get the baby in there?"

"Oh, boy. We'll have to talk about that one later."

Before I got pregnant, I was still a kid myself and living life irresponsibly, not planning for the future, living for the moment. After Brittany was born, I had to learn how to be a mom and how to make adult decisions. Suddenly, I was responsible for another person's life, and that experience forced me to grow up.

Before I had children, I had no idea how deep love can grow—and now I am better able to understand God's love for me. When I feel concern for my girls, when I delight in them, I realize that God feels those same emotions toward me. He loves me unconditionally, just as I love my children.

Single mom

My life as a single mother was one roller coaster ride after another. I was tough and determined, but I was also young, inexperienced, and broke.

Fortunately, I have always been an independent person. I got my first official job when I was in tenth grade. I worked at a campground, stacking wood for campsites, cleaning restrooms and the like. At my school, if you had a job they would let you out early, so as soon as I finished my classes, I'd go to work. I also babysat and cleaned houses whenever I could—my parents just didn't have money to give me, so I had to earn what I needed.

I had put myself through Pearl River with the help of a basketball scholarship, and I decided I would take whatever job I had to in order to support myself and Brittany. But even though I was determined and willing to work hard, I quickly found out what it's like to barely make the rent payment each month.

After Brittany was born, a bank hired me to work in their collections department. I sat in a little gray cubicle and called people whose mortgages or loans were about to go into foreclosure. The people I called would inevitably launch into a story about their sick children or invalid mothers. My heart would break, of course, because I could relate to their problems.

I remember getting a call from a man who told me he was a single dad. "I'm sorry I'm late with my payments," he said. "I'm not a deadbeat, but I've got to take care of my kid. Surely you understand that."

Did I ever. But I also had a job to do.

"Could you send half a payment?" I asked. "Or even half of a half?"

At the same time I was begging people to pay their bills, I could barely afford my own apartment, groceries, and diapers for Brittany. My parents and Brett's parents helped when they could, but I wanted to be responsible for myself. One day I typed my own account number into the bank's computer and was horrified to see that I had bounced six checks—not exactly a good thing for a bank employee to do. You'd think that someone with barely any money in the bank would find it easy to keep track of her mostly non-existent income, but my bills were always bigger than my paycheck.

When I left the job at the bank, I was hired as a waitress at a local country club. I drove the beverage cart out to the golfers and worked in the cocktail lounge.

My first week on the job, I was sent to take the drink order for a table of eight. I was still inexperienced and nervous. I smoothed my hair, adjusted my smile, and approached them.

"Hello, I'm Deanna, and I'll be taking your order today. Can I start you off with something to drink?"

"Rum and Coke," said the first man.

I nodded and smiled at the next customer. "And you, sir?"

I listened to all of their requests, told them I'd be right back, and headed toward the bar. "Hey," I told the bartender, "I've got drink orders."

"Okay." He braced his hands on the counter. "What'll they have?"

I tilted my head. "I don't know."

I had been so overwhelmed by the large group that I'd forgotten to write down the order. I had to go back and ask everyone again.

I mostly worked weekends while waitressing, and my mom and Brett's mom, Bonita, helped me out by taking care of Britt while I worked.

The hardest thing about single parenthood is the dead-end feeling that can seem overwhelming at times. You're strapped financially, yet you're always on your way to work, to school, or to the day care center. You want to spend time with your children, but you have to invest hours away from them in order to make ends meet. It's easy to feel that you're never making any progress, or that you've reached a dead end. There's never enough money for groceries and rent and day care and college and auto insurance, and unless you have a great medical plan at work, you can forget about health insurance. What are you supposed to do if you get sick?

Not only do you worry about money, but you worry about whether or not you're doing enough for your children. Are they getting enough love and attention? Do they feel secure in the home you're struggling to provide? I don't know what I would have done if my mom and Brett's mom hadn't been there to pick up the slack for me. Having two willing grandmothers nearby was such a tremendous blessing for Brittany and me.

So, how do you manage?

Every morning you pick yourself up and tell yourself that there is an end in sight. Things will get better. You will eventually finish that degree and you will get a better job. There are so many opportunities out there that you can't let yourself get stuck in a rut. Don't let yourself indulge in a pity party. Instead, find help when you need it, and find the thing that works for you and allows you to make ends meet.

Above all, remember this: you are not alone.

Single parenthood was definitely not easy, and I have a great deal of respect for people who manage to work, take care of their children, and finish college.

When Brittany was still quite small, I decided to postpone college so I could work full-time. I got a job at a chiropractor's office, and I would drop Britt off at the Favres' before heading to work. Bonita took Britt to "The Hawk's Nest," a day care program at the high school where she worked. She always tried to walk Britt to class, but Britt would say, "I'm a big girl, I can go myself." So Bonita would wait for her to turn the corners and then follow her to make sure she got to class safely.

In February 1992, when Brett was traded from the Atlanta Falcons to the Green Bay Packers in exchange for a first-round draft pick, he wanted me to go back to school full-time and not work—which was a real blessing to me. I was able to finish my courses and graduate with a degree in exercise science.

Making the most of an opportunity

Brett saw his first real action with the Packers that fall, during a home game against the Cincinnati Bengals.

As luck would have it, I had traveled to the game from Mississippi to visit Brett. In the airport, I met three cops from Long Island and they asked me why I was going to Green Bay. When I told them I was dating the Packers' backup quarterback, Brett Favre, they graciously offered me a ride once we landed.

The morning of the game, I told Brett, "Good luck!" and he said, "For what?" I told him, "You never know." As it happened, midway through the first quarter, Green Bay's starting quarterback, Don Majkowski, got hurt, and Brett was sent into the game. I was so excited and nervous for him! Of course, I felt terrible for Don—I would never wish an injury on anyone.

Brett struggled for the first couple of plays, and some of the fans were chanting for Ty Detmer, the third-string quarterback, to go in. But Brett hung in there and led the Packers to a great come-from-behind victory. The highlight of the game was a five-play, ninety-two-yard drive in the fourth quarter that ended with a thirty-five-yard touchdown pass with only thirteen seconds left in the game. That pass gave the Packers a 24–23 victory and gave Brett the starting job at quarterback. Fifteen years later, he has yet to miss a single game.

I was so proud of him that day—and thrilled that I was actually able to be there! I often wonder about my three cop friends from Long Island. I like to believe they were just as excited for us as I was.

Back then, I couldn't have known how well Brett would do in the National Football League, but I believed in him. Belief in him came naturally, because I'd done it ever since we were kids.

losing yards

In November 1992, in a game against Philadelphia, Brett took a terrible pounding. He was sacked three times by the Eagles' Reggie White and separated his shoulder. The pain was bad enough that he was given an injection of Novocain at halftime, but he stayed in the game, impressing his teammates—*and* Reggie White, who signed with the Packers as a free agent the next spring.

After that bone-jarring day, Brett did something he'd never done before. He took Vicodin, a prescribed painkiller. The pain went away.

That one use, and a couple of subsequent uses, weren't the cause of Brett's addiction to Vicodin. Those problems began months later, when he was nursing a hangover after a victory celebration. He took a few "Vikes" that someone gave him, and his headache went away.

Brett always says that no one else is to blame for his drug problem, and no particular person was his supplier. For a couple of years, he popped a few pills when he had aches and pains (which was fairly often, considering his job), but by 1994 he was craving the pills. And even though Vicodin wreaked havoc on his stomach, he learned how to compensate for the unpleasant effects.

When Brett came home to Mississippi the next summer, he had hernia surgery to repair a torn muscle in his side. The doctor prescribed Vicodin, and Brett felt grateful to have a legitimate prescription. Unfortunately, he kept complaining of pain long after the surgery, and the doctor kept refilling the prescription.

During the off-season, Brett asked me to join him in Green Bay. I decided that Brittany and I would move in with him to see if Brett and I were ready for what we hadn't been ready for as teenagers: marriage. Brett owned a four-bedroom house about five minutes from the football field, and I was actually excited about moving up there and becoming a family. We had been dating off and on for eleven years, so we saw the coming season as a "make it or break it" time for us.

Brett kissed me good-bye as he left Hattiesburg for a minicamp in Green Bay, and I promised to follow a couple of months later, lugging all my stuff and Brittany's along with me.

When I arrived in Green Bay, at first I thought everything was going to be okay. I enrolled Brittany in the first grade, and she was in heaven, thrilled to be living with her daddy. But after a few weeks, I began to realize that Brett was no longer the man I knew.

After a few weeks, I began to realize that Brett was no longer the man I knew.

The Brett I knew was quiet; this Brett was a party boy who stayed out all night with his friends. He was loud, rough, and often hateful. I saw the first signs of a mean streak I didn't know Brett had.

I wasn't sure what had changed him, but I suspected it had something to do with drugs or alcohol.

Brett didn't seem to care that Brittany and I were in the house. He started to ignore us soon after we arrived, and when I pressed him on it, he became very snappish with me. I kept wondering if I should go back home, because this life was not at all what I had expected. It didn't take long before our "make it or break it" year began to look like "break it."

I noticed other things about Brett, too. After I had my wisdom teeth removed, he asked me to call my dentist and say my mouth was sore. "Why?" I asked. "My teeth are fine."

"Because," he said, "my back is killing me and there's no other way to get pain pills."

Because Brett wasn't a liar, I believed him. What I didn't know was that he was using everyone he knew—me, the team doctors, his trainers, and his teammates—to get pain-killers. Anyone who might have Vicodin, or access to it, became a target. He had no trouble getting the drug, because he worked in a job where people get hurt all the time. Professional athletes live with pain.

Brett also had mood swings that he'd never displayed before. He'd either be mean and hateful, or he'd go out with his friends and ignore me altogether. He'd be fine when he came home from work and we had dinner, but as the evening wore on he'd become distant and surly. Or he'd leave us at home without saying a word about where he was going.

One day, I stepped into our closet and found a plastic bag filled with white pills. Brett was always getting banged up in practice and in games, so I wasn't surprised to see that he had painkillers on hand. I knew they were Vicodin, because the name was right on the pill, but why were they in a bag instead of a prescription bottle?

I began to notice that Brett didn't need as much sleep as an ordinary person—in fact, he behaved like some kind of high-strung superman. He'd stay up until three or four in the morning and then get up at seven and go to work. He was drinking, too, more heavily than I'd ever seen him drink. I couldn't understand how a man could drink, party, and work as hard as he did. The few times I went out with him and his friends, I could barely pull myself out of bed the next morning. I knew he was strong, but he wasn't Superman.

Finally, I came right out and asked him if he was abusing painkillers. He got defensive and wouldn't even consider that he might have a problem.

I went to my friend Gayle, the wife of quarterbacks coach Steve Mariucci, and said, "I think Brett has a problem." Gayle talked to Steve, and Steve confronted Brett, who became angry and said I was crazy. "It's not true; I'm not doing that," he said. When Brett came home, he blasted me for talking to Gayle. "You don't know what you're talking about," he told me. "I'm not on drugs."

Brett was never physically abusive to me, but like the typical addict in denial, he tried to turn the situation around and make everything my fault.

Dangerous denial

Meanwhile, I became depressed. I'd left my home in Mississippi, my family, and my friends, and I was homesick and lonely. With the way things were going with Brett, I didn't want to stay in Green Bay. The only reason I stayed was because Brittany had entered first grade and I didn't want to pull her out of school in the middle of the year.

As the situation became worse and Brett grew more withdrawn, I talked to his mom and his agent. They each spoke to Brett, and like before, he denied that he had a problem. Everyone knew that quarterbacks take a pounding in the NFL, and Brett admitted that he took painkillers after games, but he kept insisting adamantly that he didn't have a problem. As time went on, he became increasingly defensive and distant with me.

I had never known anyone with a drug problem, so I didn't know how to cope. I told myself things were okay, that maybe he was just using the pills during the season. Furthermore, I didn't want to tell anyone else about his problem. I didn't want my family to know I was going through such a tough time. I didn't want them to worry about me all alone up there in Green Bay.

I did ask a couple of my friends, Pam and Kent Johnston, to pray for us. Sometimes, I'd go to their house two times a week and we'd pray together.

The Green Bay Packers had some dynamite Christians on the team. Reggie White would often try to talk to the guys, but when you don't want to hear about your destructive lifestyle, you tend to avoid situations where the subject might come up. Brett loved and respected Reggie, but he would never put himself in a place where he'd have to listen to straight talk from the Minister of Defense. Reggie was bold and never hesitated to tell the other players to straighten up. Sometimes his wife would tell me, "Reggie's talking to those boys," but what he was saying didn't seem to affect Brett. Either that, or Brett wasn't listening.

When I tried to tell people that I thought Brett had a serious problem, no one could understand how he could be abusing alcohol and drugs and yet play so well. He was such a good player that no one wanted to believe he had an addiction. When

I talked to other family members, his agent, and anyone else I hoped might listen, they thought I was only feeling insecure and trying to save the relationship. There were other women at those places where Brett and his friends were partying, so most people assumed I was jealous and simply wanted him to stop going out. But I knew something was dreadfully wrong.

One night, I walked into the room and heard Brett talking on the phone to a woman I had discovered he'd been calling. "That's it," I told him, "I don't deserve to be treated like this. You asked me to move up here to Green Bay and now you're calling these girls—well, you're on your own now. I'm not living this way. All this stuff is over for me."

I had sacrificed a lot to stay in Green Bay and to try to support him, but he didn't acknowledge my sacrifices. I'm not sure he even recognized them. But now he heard the finality in my voice and realized I was done. Finished.

The next day, he sent me flowers and begged me not to go. I talked to Gayle Mariucci and told her I was going to leave Brett and go back to Mississippi. I had endured all I could, and though I still loved him, I couldn't take any more.

Gayle heard me out, and she was worried about Brett's well-being. "Don't leave," she said, "or Brett will end up killing himself. All the guys are having a great time being with him, but none of them know him like you do. They don't know that they're not seeing the real Brett."

At that point, I knew she was right. If I left and Brett kept using drugs, he was going to kill himself. And even though I couldn't stop him, I thought it was my responsibility to stick around and do everything I could to try to fix him. Now I can see that all my efforts only enabled him to keep using the drugs. I learned the hard way that sometimes the only way to help a drug addict is through tough love.

Performer of the year

On February 12, 1996, Brett and I flew to New York to attend the ESPY Awards, where Brett was to receive an award as pro football's Performer of the Year. We were both excited when Dennis Hopper made the presentation. What I didn't know was that the entire time Brett was on stage giving his acceptance speech, he had a bottle of Vicodin tucked in his pants pocket.

After receiving his trophy, Brett went backstage for pictures and then came back to his seat next to me to watch the rest of the ceremony. After the show, we went to the "after party," where we got to hang out with celebrities like Kevin Nealon, Grant Aleksander and his wife, Sherry, and others, but around ten o'clock, Brett started getting antsy. Finally, he leaned over and whispered to me: "I'll be back. I'm going to the bathroom."

He got up and left me sitting there . . . for over an hour.

You can imagine what I felt. I kept trying to smile and keep up conversations with all of these important people, but all the while my mind was preoccupied with the whereabouts of my missing boyfriend. I turned my head and tried not to be obvious about scanning the crowd. Was Brett all right? Or had he been waylaid by a band of overzealous autograph hounds?

I had never felt more alone in my entire life.

I didn't know—didn't dream—that he was in the bathroom swallowing pills. Later I learned that it took him twenty minutes just to swallow about fifteen pills, because he kept throwing up. He kept peeking over the stall to be sure he was alone, then he'd choke down more pills.

When he finally had the drugs in his system, he went

outside, posed for pictures with Dennis Hopper, and then walked around feeling the Vicodin buzz. He went manic when the drugs hit him, so he was talking his fool head off.

By the time he got back to our group, I wasn't worried—I was ticked off. Worse yet, when I looked at him, I knew he was wired on something.

"Did you take something?" I hissed.

He shook his head, but I knew he was lying. And Brett had never been a liar—until then.

The next day, Brett flew off to Mississippi, where he was living during the off-season, and I returned to Green Bay so Brittany could finish first grade with her class. (At the time, I had no idea that players would split schools with their kids during and after the season.) Throughout the flight, I kept asking myself why I was sticking around. Brett didn't care about me anymore. He didn't pay any attention to me. It seemed like we were going in different directions. I was ready to pack up and go home, but I still didn't want to pull Brittany out of school before the end of the year.

I had never felt more alone in my entire life.

fumble and recovery

One night, I got a call from Mississippi—Brett was in the emergency room because he'd had a panic attack. A *what*? I'd never in my life known anybody less likely to panic than Brett. Then I learned that he was okay, and he was leaving the hospital with Vicodin and a prescription for three refills.

That's when I realized the depth of his problem. He must have specifically asked for the Vicodin and the refills.

I truly believe that Brett might have destroyed himself if not for a single day toward the end of February 1996. They say God works in mysterious ways, and on that cold February day, nothing was more mysterious than the seizure Brett suffered after what should have been a routine operation to remove bone spurs from his ankle.

Brett had come back to Green Bay to have surgery on his ankle, and Brittany and I were excited about going to visit him in the hospital. Dr. Pat McKenzie, one of the team's physicians, had done the surgery, and he assured us it would be no big deal. With the bone spur gone, Brett would stop feeling some discomfort he'd had during the past season.

When we got to the hospital, we were relieved to hear that Brett had come through the operation with flying colors. The anesthesia had made him nauseated, but that wasn't unusual.

He was awake when we sailed into the room. I kissed him and then helped Brittany climb onto the bed. She was careful not to touch his leg, but I know she felt better just knowing her daddy was okay.

As Britt stretched out next to Brett and grabbed the television remote, I moved to the foot of the bed and studied the dressings on his foot. "Are you in pain?"

Brett shook his head and shot me a goofy grin. "I'm not feeling anything."

A nurse came in to check his IV. I tensed, knowing how much Brett hates needles. As the nurse took his hand to pull the needle out of his vein, Brett looked at me and rolled his eyes, his way of telling me that he'd just as soon do without needles of any kind.

Then his eyes rolled again—only this time they rolled back in his head. I stared, amazed that he'd be goofing off so soon after surgery, and then I saw his arms and legs begin to tremble.

He was having a seizure.

As the nurse began to attend to Brett, my mind flashed to that old saying that someone having a seizure could swallow their tongue. I'm not sure that's even possible, but at that moment, all I could think of was, *What if his tongue blocks his airway!*

As Brett flailed in his bed, senseless, I pulled Brittany to my side and tried to shield her eyes. As more help came on the run, I hustled Brittany out of the room, but not before her eyes filled with tears. "Is he going to die, Mommy?"

Once the doctors had stabilized Brett, they told me they would examine him and run some tests. When the results of the blood work came back a few hours later, the doctors told Brett he had a toxic liver.

Long story short: circumstances forced Brett to tell his doctors—and the NFL—about the Vicodin, and he voluntarily admitted himself to the NFL's drug rehab program.

Signing up for rehab

When Brett announced his addiction publicly and said he was going into rehab, I breathed a simple prayer: "Thank you, God."

As he entered the Menninger Clinic in Topeka for a month and a half of treatment, I prepared to host the first annual Brett Favre Celebrity Golf Tournament in Gulfport, Mississippi, in his absence.

While Brett was in Kansas, he received help for more than just his drug problem. He was able to talk to a counselor there about the different choices he'd made in his life, and the consequences of those choices. He had time to think about our relationship—what we'd been through together, where we were, and where we were headed. He decided that he really wanted to turn his life around, and he wanted us to stay together.

We spoke on the phone while he was at the clinic, and for the first time in a long time, he mentioned marriage. I said, "I'm not sure we should be talking about that right now." At that point, I wasn't sure I wanted to be married to Brett Favre. I loved him as much as ever, but I didn't want to watch him self-destruct. For so long, I had prayed and prayed for him to change, and now I was thinking that it couldn't have just happened overnight.

Also, during those years in Green Bay when our relationship was under so much stress, I had begun making plans to further my education. As I came to believe that my relationship with Brett was a dead-end street, I saw furthering my education as a way to remain independent and take care of myself. And it was a way to pursue something that interested me.

I wasn't sure I wanted to be married to Brett Favre. I loved him as much as ever, but I didn't want to watch him self-destruct.

When I first started college, I thought I might like to be a coach, but everyone had told me I wouldn't make any money as a coach for women's athletics. "Be a nurse," they said, "because you'll always have a job and you'll make good money." After finishing community college, I had been accepted to the nursing program at the University of Southern Mississippi, but I'd quickly realized that nursing was not my cup of tea. I love helping others, but I have a weak stomach. Certain smells—like that "hospital smell"—make me nauseated, and shots make me queasy. I just didn't do well with all that.

The nursing curriculum, however, included a class on nutrition, and I found that it fascinated me. I learned what a registered dietitian does and realized that I'd love to help people lose weight and stay healthy through nutrition and fitness. So after I completed my degree in exercise science at USM, I decided to continue my studies in dietetics.

While I was waiting for Brittany to finish first grade in Green Bay, I applied to the dietetics program at USM. Only sixteen people would be admitted into the program, and I had to gather letters of recommendation and be interviewed by a panel in order to be considered. When I got the letter saying I'd been accepted, I was amazed and excited. I was ready to go. I was ready to move on.

I think Brett realized that we had come to a crossroads in our lives. He knew if I went home to Hattiesburg and enrolled at USM, I would probably never come back.

Not finished with darkness

When Brett came home from the Menninger Clinic, I hoped and prayed that his substance abuse problems were all in the past. He had completely stopped taking Vicodin, but he still wanted to be able to drink alcohol when he was out with the guys. Drinking made him feel more at ease in groups (and football players can always draw a crowd). I knew that Brett wasn't going to be able to drink like he used to—after all, alcohol is just another drug. But he thought he could still drink on weekends and at social events. The NFL's substance-abuse program, however, required him to stop drinking for two years. Because drinking impairs judgment, they know someone addicted to any substance is more likely to relapse if he continues to use alcohol.

As soon as Brett came out of rehab, he asked me again to marry him. "I'm really serious," he said. He told me about the counseling he'd received at the clinic; I had gone to Topeka myself to sit in on a couple of his sessions, so I had seen first-hand what he was learning. Still, I wasn't sure that he was ready—or that I was.

A friend of mine had told me a story that really resonated with me. The teenage daughter of a family had made a decision to lie to her parents. When her dad found out about the lie, he didn't say anything at first. Instead, he waited until the family was seated at the dinner table one night, and then he got up and took a beautiful and rare piece of china from the hutch. While the mother and daughter watched, he slammed the china onto the floor, where it broke into dozens of jagged pieces.

Then the dad looked at the daughter and said, "You know that thing called trust? That's what you've done to it. All those little pieces—how can you put that back together?"

After three or four years of Brett's drug problems, the trust in our relationship was in a lot of little pieces. That didn't mean it was beyond repair, but it was going to take some work. You can mend broken trust, but it's not easy. Both parties must commit to the goal of renewing the injured relationship.

After Brett came home, for the first time in a long time I began to see his willingness to make our relationship work. He was attentive again, willing to compromise, and it was as if he had finally realized that he couldn't always count on *me* to make the sacrifices; *he* had to make some too. I had needs that needed to be met, and he had to be willing to do his part in our relationship.

I began to see a change in him. Instead of just going out the door to do whatever he wanted to do, he'd discuss it with me or ask if I thought it was a good idea. I began to feel like a partner instead of his caretaker. I began to feel loved again.

In high school, we had been inseparable. Both of us were shy, and though we weren't exactly antisocial, we didn't do a lot with other people. I had a couple of good friends, but Brett was always either with me or with his family.

When he went to college, he'd had to cope with starting out in a new place, being a freshman, and facing all those guys on the team who had been there a long time. He wasn't sure how he should fit in, and that's when he had turned to drinking. He became a different person, and everybody soon began to think he was Mr. Wild Man, a real party animal. Brett is a funny guy, but he's even funnier when he's filled with "liquid courage." Once he got a taste of that life, he wanted to be out partying all the time.

When I moved up to Green Bay, I wanted to spend time with him, but I wasn't always welcome when he was out with the guys. He wanted me to be around at his convenience, but not when he was out having a good time with his friends. He had become someone I didn't know at all.

But now, as I watched and listened to him open his heart, and as I saw his commitment to making our relationship work, I looked at him with tears in my eyes and saw the young man I'd known in Mississippi. I whispered, "My old Brett's back." And then I told him that yes, I'd marry him.

I ended up writing a letter to decline my spot in the dietetics program. It was one of the hardest things I've ever had to do, and one of the most difficult sacrifices I've ever made. I wanted it so badly, but I believed in Brett more, and I wanted to be with him.

Because the opening of training camp was rapidly approaching, we realized that if we wanted to get married we had better do it right away. Brett set everything in motion by being the first to go to the courthouse to sign the marriage license. That's when I *knew* he was serious. With no time to lose, I contacted Father Getchel at St. Agnes Catholic Church in Green Bay and asked, "Will you marry Brett and me next Sunday?" Fortunately, he was available. That meant we had exactly one week to get my dress and the rings and make all the other arrangements.

I didn't care about having a big wedding and the perfect dress. I was far more concerned about what the wedding stands for—the vows made before God and man—than the frills that go along with a typical wedding.

On July 14, 1996, Brett and I were married in a simple ceremony at St. Agnes. Kent Johnston, Brett's friend and the Packers' strength coach, was best man. Kent's wife, Pam, was my matron of honor. Brett's mom and my mom flew up for the ceremony, but unfortunately, because things were so rushed, not all of our family members were able to make it. To this day, one of my biggest regrets is that my sister, Christie, wasn't able to be there with me. Brittany was our flower girl, and she was ecstatic. On the way to the church, she looked at me and said, "This makes me *so* happy!"

Pam, my matron of honor, offered to bake our wedding cake, but I was skeptical. Pam is very athletic, a power lifter—not the sort you'd imagine moonlighting in a bakery. "I don't know," I told her, not at all certain she could do it, "but if you want to try, go ahead."

Was I ever surprised! She baked a two-tiered amaretto-raspberry cake that was the most beautiful creation I'd ever seen.

Brett had to report to training camp the day after the wedding, so he and I honeymooned in Kohler, Wisconsin, a beautiful little village about sixty miles from Green Bay, because there wasn't time to go to Hawaii or someplace more exotic.

On the first day of training camp, the Packers set up a press conference for Brett to answer questions about his time in rehab. He read a statement saying that he had suffered from a dependency to painkillers, but that he had been cleared by the experts and no longer had a dependency to Vicodin or any other pain medication.

"Further," he read, "it has been rumored that my problems also involve alcoholism. The same specialist stated unequivocally that I do not have a problem in this area, namely that I am not an alcoholic. . . . I realize that while I am in this program, I must abstain from alcohol. I am aware that I have an obligation, not only to myself but also to my fans and team, to comply with the rules while in this system. Others have faced tougher trials and succeeded."

When a reporter asked Brett if he was worried about suffering a relapse, he answered, "All I can tell people is, 'If you don't believe me, bet against me'—because eventually they'll lose. I'm going to beat this thing. I'm going to win the Super Bowl."[1]

I don't know whether the reporters believed Brett, but I did.

Emotional roller coaster

After Brett and I married in 1996, we wanted to enlarge our family right away. Little did we know that getting pregnant would prove to be a lot more difficult than it had been the first time.

Three months after the wedding, I participated in a fashion show featuring several players' wives. A friend and I were standing in line, waiting to go on, when another woman came up and gave me a sly smile. Without batting an eye, she said, "You look really good for being three months pregnant."

Excuse me? You could have knocked me over with a feather. Apparently that was one of the rumors circulating around town—that Brett and I had gotten married because we had to.

In hindsight, that's almost funny. If we had wanted to get married because we *had* to, we'd have gotten married when I discovered I was pregnant with Brittany. And given the rocky road we'd traveled since then, we probably wouldn't be together.

For two years, I rode the emotional roller coaster every infertile woman knows. I watched the calendar, analyzed every queasy moment in hopes it might be morning sickness, and refrained from taking any medications if I even suspected I might be pregnant. I would get my hopes up—*maybe, finally, this time*—only to have them dashed again and again.

Nearly two years after our wedding, I still wasn't pregnant, and I could hear my biological clock ticking. Brett and I both went to the doctor to be checked out, and the experts found no serious medical problems. Then, in late 1997, I was rushed to the hospital with severe abdominal pains. When they did surgery to remove a couple of cysts, they discovered I had severe endometriosis, a condition that results when endometrial tissue is found outside the uterus. I went to a specialist, who examined me and said that she thought I should be able to get pregnant. So, for several more months, we followed the routine known to so many couples—ovulation predictors, temperature readings, a careful monitoring of the calendar. Nothing stifles romance and enhances desperation like infertility.

I could almost laugh at the irony. How could someone have an unexpected pregnancy when she's a teenager and not be able to conceive when she's married, settled, and eager to expand her family?

In vitro miracle

By the fall of 1998, we were ready to try a more scientific approach. One of my doctors had suggested in vitro fertilization, but before I would even consider it, I wanted to be certain the procedure was something a Christian could attempt in good conscience. I called my priest to ask his opinion, and he said, "I think God has blessed us with technology. If you want to choose that route, it's okay."

I felt that as long as we didn't deliberately destroy fertilized eggs—embryos—we would be proceeding in an effort to increase our family and uphold the sanctity of life. I would never ignore or sanction the destruction of embryos, because they are human lives, created in the image of God just as I am. I've heard some people say that human life doesn't begin until the child is born, but I don't believe that. The egg and sperm are alive before they even unite. Life is a gift passed on from mother and father, a gift that ultimately springs from the hand of God. God first breathed life into Adam in the Garden of Eden, and we've been giving our children the gift of life ever since.

I could almost laugh at the irony. How could someone have an unexpected pregnancy when she's a teenager and not be able to conceive when she's married, settled, and eager to expand her family?

The in vitro process proved to be neither pleasant nor easy. I had to take subcutaneous shots in my abdomen, and Brett—who doesn't like needles or blood work of any kind—had to administer the injections. They gave me Lupron to "turn off" my normal menstrual cycle, so at the age of twenty-nine, I went through a sort of induced menopause, including hot flashes and night sweats.

I remember waking in the middle of the night with my hair drenched and the bed soaked. I got up, preparing to change my pajamas and pull out some dry linens, when Brett woke up. "D," he asked, feeling the damp sheets, "did you wet the bed?"

I wanted to throw a pillow at him.

When the Lupron injections had eradicated my natural hormones, they gave me another drug to make my ovaries produce more follicles, which are the egg-containing areas inside the ovary. There are hundreds of thousands of follicles in every woman's ovaries, but during any one cycle only a few will grow large enough to appear on an ultrasound, and only the large follicles hold mature eggs. In a normal menstrual cycle, only one follicle matures, but the fertility specialists gave me a concentrated form of natural hormones, called gonadotropins, to stimulate ovulation so that several follicles would enlarge at once.

When the follicles reach a certain size, a technician retrieves the eggs. When my doctors performed this procedure, I had six eggs that were mature enough to use. Of the six, only four fertilized, so I asked the doctors to transfer all four to my uterus. Three is the recommended number, but I didn't want to leave one out, nor did I want to destroy a human life.

After the four eggs were transferred, I went home and held my breath, hoping they would grow into the children Brett and I wanted so badly. Quadruplets would have been a challenge, but we were up for it.

Three weeks passed before the clinic would confirm that the in vitro had been successful. My levels of HCG (the hormone they look for to indicate pregnancy) remained low for the first two weeks, but then they shot up and the nurse told me I was officially pregnant. Two of the embryos had implanted, but one eventually died. The other, however, grew strong.

This pregnancy wasn't as easy as my first. I gained a little more weight, and I was nauseated around the clock during the first four months. But that discomfort was minor compared to the joy that followed.

Our second baby girl was born in July 1999, and we named her Breleigh Ann. (Brett's mother, my mother, Brett's sister, and my sister all share the middle name Ann.) She arrived five weeks early, but she was healthy and beautiful at five pounds, seven ounces, and seventeen inches long. With two girls, Brett and I counted ourselves blessed indeed.

Later, we tried in vitro a second time, but none of the embryos survived. In hindsight, I can see evidence of God's wisdom even in that sorrow. If the second embryo transfer had succeeded, I would have been pregnant at the time I was battling an aggressive cancer. If the cancer had been estrogen-related, a pregnancy would have made the tumor grow even faster.

Now that we're in our late thirties, Brett and I believe we have the family God intended for us to have. People are always asking Brett if he wanted a son, but he adores our girls and he knows it would be hard to be the son of a three-time NFL MVP. People would have placed incredible pressure on any son we might have had, and we wouldn't want that for any of our children.

As our girls have grown, Brett and I have seen ourselves in each of them. Brittany is quiet and reserved, more like me. When I was young, people always said I looked serious, but I couldn't help it; I was just reserved and laid back. Britt's a lot like that, more quiet and reserved than a lot of people. She's low key—not loud or dramatic.

Breleigh, on the other hand, is very dramatic and animated, and she loves excitement. Like Brett, she is sensitive, loves to tell funny stories, and is always very concerned about things. She's into dance, cheerleading, and acting.

Last year, we hosted a fund-raising dinner for the Brett Favre Fourward Foundation to benefit disadvantaged and disabled children in Wisconsin. I was the speaker, and Brett was also going to get up and say a few words, so we had a microphone set up. Brittany wanted nothing to do with that microphone, but Breleigh, who was seven, really wanted to say something. She worried herself to death about that microphone until I told her she could say something; then she worried about what she should say. Finally, I told Brett to take her up to the mike, and I told Breleigh to say, "Thank you so much for coming; it was a good evening." She recited it perfectly, and it was hilarious.

Then Brittany looked at me and said, "I can't believe she wanted to do that." Our girls are complete opposites, but they're both such a blessing.

Not only do I have two precious girls, but my husband also is an amazing father. He's so good with the girls. Teenage daughters and their moms often have struggles, but when Brittany and I have a disagreement, Brett can go into her room and talk without ever becoming angry. He can explain my position in a way that Britt can understand, and they never fight. It's phenomenal how good he is at smoothing over a conflict. I'm amazed that the toughest man in football can be such a sensitive father.

God knew what he was doing when he sent our girls to us—just as he knew what he was doing when he brought Brett and me together.

God knew what he was doing when he sent our girls to us—just as he knew what he was doing when he brought Brett and me together. As Brett's wife, I want to be his confidante and the best friend that he needs. I want him to know that I'll always be on his side, no matter what. I try to express my feelings often so he'll know how much I love and admire him. Obviously, there are some things a husband can do to shake a marriage, but I don't worry about Brett now. There's nothing but love and trust between us today.

sudden death

I don't know whether you're familiar with the biblical story of Job, but as I look back over the past ten years, I find myself sympathizing with the man. Job went from living on a mountaintop to dwelling in the valley—and I'm not referring to geography.

Job had troubles—the kind of trials I wouldn't wish on anyone—yet God allowed him to suffer. He had his reasons for Job's troubles, and I know he has reasons for mine.

The Bible tells us that Job lived a blameless life; he feared God and stayed away from evil. He raised a close-knit family that included seven sons and three daughters, and he was the wealthiest person in town.

But one day Satan appeared before God and said, "'Job has good reason to fear [you]. You have always put a wall of protection around him and his home and his property. You have made him prosper in everything he does. Look how rich he is! But reach out and take away everything he has, and he will surely curse you to your face!'

"'All right, you may test him,' the LORD said to Satan. 'Do whatever you want with everything he possesses, but don't harm him physically.'"[1]

Shortly thereafter, an enemy raided Job's fields. All his animals, the source of his wealth, were stolen, and all his servants were killed. To make matters worse, all ten of Job's beloved children were feasting in the oldest son's home when the house collapsed. In one tragic hour, Job lost all his children.

When Job heard the dreadful news, he tore his clothes. He wept in sorrow, but instead of yelling at God, he lifted his gaze to heaven and said, "The LORD gave me what I had, and the LORD has taken it away. Praise the name of the LORD!"[2]

I wouldn't want you to think I'm as virtuous as Job, and I haven't lost everything in a single hour. But, like Job, I know what it's like to wake up one morning with no real problems and to crawl into bed that night under a crushing weight of grief.

Unexpected sorrow

Though the Packers' loss in Super Bowl XXXII was a low moment for our family, the following years brought more blessings than we could count: a lovely home where we could put down roots, a lifetime contract for Brett with the Packers, and the continued love and support of our families. We weren't immune to trouble—like any family, we had our ups and downs—but by 2003 we were sailing on relatively untroubled seas.

On Sunday, December 21, 2003, as I was driving home from some last-minute Christmas shopping in Green Bay, I got a call from Rhonda, my sister-in-law in Mississippi, with some bad news about Brett's dad.

"Irvin was just in a bad accident," she said. "We don't know if he's going to make it. He ran off the road near the house."

I struggled to keep my own car on the highway. "Did he hit someone?"

"We don't know what happened, but it doesn't look good."

"Are you at the hospital?"

"No," she said, "but I just talked to Jeff, and they're saying he's not going to make it."

"Call me back when you know something," I told her.

I hung up and tried to focus on my driving. This couldn't be happening. Irvin Favre was a solid man, as strong as an oak, and I couldn't imagine him being seriously hurt. There had to be some kind of mistake. Some irrational part of my brain insisted I wasn't prepared for a family tragedy. Christmas was coming and Brett was out in California, getting ready for a Monday night game against the Oakland Raiders.

As I drove, I couldn't help thinking of another accident in our family's past. The summer between Brett's junior and senior years in college, he was driving less than a mile from his parents' house when the right front tire of his Nissan Maxima hit some loose gravel on the shoulder of the road. The car shot out of control, hit a culvert, slid down an embankment, flipped three times, and smashed into a pine tree.

Brett was knocked unconscious, and when he awoke he was in the backseat and covered in glass. His brother Scott, who had been following with a friend in another car, was beating in the side window with a golf club because he couldn't get the door open to get to Brett.

The seat belt undoubtedly saved Brett's life, but when he

finally made it to the emergency room, the doctors told him he had a fractured vertebra, a lacerated liver, a severely bruised abdomen, and several abrasions. They said there was no way he'd play football in the fall.

With the opening game only six weeks away, Brett answered, "Just watch me."

He spent three days in intensive care and went home after five days in the hospital, but three weeks later, his stomach began to give him trouble. He'd eat, but he couldn't keep anything down. The doctors thought it was some kind of traumatic reaction to the accident, but Brett knew it was something worse.

When they readmitted him to the hospital, they discovered that two and a half feet of his small intestine had been crushed and had subsequently died. On August 7, Brett underwent surgery to remove that section of his intestines, and by the time he went back to school in mid-August, he had lost thirty-four pounds. Nevertheless, on September 8, only four and a half weeks after the surgery, he led the USM Golden Eagles to a 27–24 come-from-behind victory over the Alabama Crimson Tide. The team finished 8–3 that year, and Brett did well enough to establish several school records and help the team earn a spot in the All-American Bowl, where he was selected as MVP.

Remembering Brett's accident and how he had bounced back, I told myself that "Big Irv" was going to be okay. The Favre men were tough. Whatever had happened, he'd come through it.

My sister-in-law called me three more times while I was driving, and each time she gave me the same terrible news: "They don't think he's going to make it." Each time she called, I asked her, "Are you *sure*?" She was still getting updates from her husband, Jeff, so I said, "Call me back when you know something for sure."

The next time she called, she said the words I'd been dreading to hear. "He didn't make it. They think he had a heart attack and ran off the road."

The news was so shocking that at first it didn't register. Brett's dad was only fifty-eight—way too young to die. It just didn't seem right.

Maybe I was in denial; maybe I just didn't want to call Brett with the news. He and his father had always been close. Irvin had watched every game Brett played in. Brett would be on the field again in a few hours, and I didn't want him to play under a cloud of grief.

But sometimes what we want is not what we get.

The hard truth

By the time I got home, I couldn't deny the truth any longer. I didn't tell the girls for a while. I just sat on the sofa in shock, thinking, *What do I do?* I knew the story would soon make the national news. Brett was out in California, two hours behind us, and I didn't want him to hear the news from the media. I wanted to tell him before someone else did.

I knew he was on the golf course with three strong Christians—Doug Pederson, Ryan Longwell, and Josh Bidwell. Because Brett doesn't usually carry his cell phone, I called Jeannie Pederson, Doug's wife, and got her husband's cell phone number. She immediately offered to come over and pick up my girls so I could fly out to California to be with Brett.

As soon as Brett heard Doug say, "Hi, Deanna," he knew something was wrong. After I told Doug what had happened, he passed the phone to Brett and I gave him the news. When he began to cry, I asked, "Do you want me to come?" He said yes.

When Doug came back on the phone, I said, "Please comfort him and pray for him while I try to find a flight out there."

Being away from your loved one during a crisis is hard. Worse yet is having to deliver a terrible blow when you're not there to offer comfort.

Jeannie Pederson came over to pray with me and to pick up the girls. They would fly home to Mississippi the next morning, so I gave them the sad news. Breleigh was only four, so she didn't understand much of what was going on, but Brittany was really upset. I was distraught and crying, as well; the news was so shocking for all of us.

Being away from your loved one during a crisis is hard. Worse yet is having to deliver a terrible blow when you're not there to offer comfort.

Once the girls had gone, I packed a bag and climbed aboard a jet we had chartered to fly me to California. I arrived at 3:00 a.m., went to the hotel, and found Brett trying to sleep. He sat up when I came in, and we hugged for what felt like forever.

"Should I play?" he kept asking, and obviously he was torn. Would other people think it disrespectful if he played football the day after his father's death?

Anyone who thought so didn't know Irvin Favre.

"I just—I just can't imagine never seeing Dad again," Brett said, lying back with his eyes closed. "Mom and Dad have seen every one of my games since grade school."

I knew what Brett was going through. I had been a part of his family for years and was well aware of how tightly knit the Favre clan was. Brett, Scott, Jeff, Brandi, Bonita, and Irvin were nearly always together, whether at games, at school, or at home. Irvin's absence would leave a hole that no one else could ever fill.

I looked into my husband's red-rimmed eyes and spoke from my heart: "Your dad was so proud of you, Brett. He came to every one of your college games and has watched all of your pro games—do you think he'd want you to sit out tomorrow? I'm convinced he would have wanted you to play."

We fell asleep holding each other.

The next morning, Brett had a couple of meetings, so I went down to the locker room to see him right before the game. I could tell he was still worried about the game, and I sensed his biggest fear was that he would play, but not play well. If he played, he wanted the game to be a tribute to his dad.

"You know what?" I told him, gripping his arm. "The most fun I've ever seen your dad have were those games when you were smiling and running around and having a good time. He loved seeing you be passionate about what you're doing. The little boy that comes out of you on the field—your playing brought that out in *him*. So, play tonight. Play for him."

That was all I could think to say, but it was enough. As I watched Brett turn to face his teammates, I prayed and hoped I wouldn't regret that I had urged him to play.

A fitting tribute

The fans in Oakland are known for being rough on the visiting team, and I knew Brett was in a fragile state of mind. I'm always concerned about injuries on the field, but I was even more concerned at this game. Would Brett be so preoccupied with his grief that he wouldn't be able to keep his mind in the game? A player can be hurt in a distracted moment—and every man on the opposing defense is usually out to cream the quarterback.

I was also concerned about fallout in the press. I knew some people would criticize Brett for not rushing home to Mississippi to be with his family, but even his mom encouraged him to stay and play. If he had gone home, others would've criticized him for pulling out of a big game when his team needed him. If the Packers were going to make the playoffs, they needed to win this game against the Raiders.

In the locker room, Brett told the team that he had their backs. He said he would stay for his "Packer family," but as soon as the game was over he would fly home to be with his family.

In the stadium, I sat in the box reserved for Packer board members and braced myself for the worst. But God heard my prayers. The Oakland fans couldn't have been more supportive. Many of them carried signs that said, "Brett, we're praying for you." During the pregame introductions, they gave Brett a standing ovation, an honor they rarely give their own players. During the game, the TV cameras focused on me and introduced me to a national television audience—a debut I would have preferred to make under happier circumstances.

During the game, the TV cameras focused on me and introduced me to a national television audience—a debut I would have preferred to make under happier circumstances.

The game, which Brett dedicated as a tribute to his dad, turned out to be one of the most special and amazing games Brett has ever played. Before the final quarter ended, he had thrown for 399 yards and four touchdowns. All the receivers had told him, "If you throw it anywhere near me, I'm going to catch it," but some of the catches they made that night looked like "divine intervention."

Afterward, Brett told a reporter, "I knew that my dad would have wanted me to play. I love him so much and I love this game. It's meant a great deal to me, to my dad, to my family, and I didn't expect this kind of performance. But I know he was watching tonight."[3]

Head coach Mike Sherman told the media, "Adversity strikes all of us. It's not the adversity that affects you; it's how you handle it. And [Brett] handles adversity extremely well. His focus and concentration on this football game this evening was extraordinary. When he puts his mind to anything, even off the field, he can accomplish anything he wants to accomplish."[4]

When I had Brett to myself after the game, I told him I was proud of him, and that I knew his dad would have been proud of him. With tears welling in my eyes, I said, "I believe that he sees you and feels how special this night is. What a special game this turned out to be. I love you."

The Packers dedicated the game ball that night to "Big Irv." An honor well deserved.

After the game, we flew to Mississippi to join our families and to lay Irvin Favre to rest. We had received a tough and unexpected blow, but God had given us the strength to weather the storm . . . and an unexpected touch of grace.

My Kodak moment

In July 2004, ESPN nominated Brett for a "Best Moment" ESPY Award for his performance in the Oakland tribute game. Representatives from ESPN phoned Brett's agent, Bus

Cook, and asked if Brett would come to the show to accept the award if he won. When Brett heard about it, he said he didn't want to do it—he would have felt too awkward accepting an award for something that had occurred as a result of his father's death. For him, it wasn't a "best moment," because he had just lost his dad.

Brett was torn up about the award, but they were determined to give it to him and they wanted someone to accept it on the show. They asked me, but I said no. Finally, they asked Brett's mother, Bonita, to come to the awards ceremony. She said she'd do it, but only if I went with her. Tongue-in-cheek, I said, "Sure, if they'll assist in flying us out and help us with hair and wardrobe." We only had one day, and I knew we couldn't accomplish this on our own.

You could have knocked me over with a feather when

TEN THINGS *a shy woman would rather do than speak in front of a crowd*

1. Have a root canal.

2. Get a Brazilian wax.

3. Walk a mile in stiletto heels.

4. Listen to a lecture on nuclear physics . . . in Greek.

5. Dust every baseboard in her house . . . on her hands and knees.

6. Volunteer to be sawed in half at a magic show.

7. Clean out the pantry.

8. Browse the hardware aisle at Home Depot.

9. Catalog the family Christmas ornaments.

10. Shave her legs.

ESPN called back and said they'd make arrangements for everything. I was shocked speechless, but I'd promised Bonita I would go, so the two of us boarded a private jet and flew off to Los Angeles.

I've already mentioned that I don't like the limelight, but there I was, about to accept an award for my husband on national television. I kept telling Brett that he needed to come—in fact, I called him on our way to the airport—but he said his mom and I could handle it just fine.

If only I'd felt as confident.

A few hours later, Bonita and I found ourselves in a Los Angeles hotel with a crew of people determined to dress us for prime time. I felt sorry for those TV people. They were used to dressing Hollywood size fours, and now they found themselves facing a couple of home-fed Mississippi girls, neither one of whom was eager to face the camera.

As the wardrobe people scrambled to find us something to wear, I took a few minutes to work on my speech, which I had written on a card. I read that card dozens of times, but I was so terrified I'd mess it up that the words just wouldn't settle in my head. I tried to memorize those few lines, but my brain went blank every time I stopped looking at the card.

Finally, the wardrobe people found a nice suit for me and a black dress for Bonita. They assured me my speech would be on a teleprompter, but I was so worried about ruining everything that I couldn't relax and enjoy the moment. We attended a rehearsal, but I was so self-conscious about the microphone that I mumbled my speech under my breath and moved away from the mike as quickly as I could.

I watched the passing hours with a sense of dread. What had I done? What in the world had possessed me to make that silly promise? My insides felt like jelly, and my hands trembled like leaves.

Before leaving the house, I had told my sister, a nurse practitioner, that I was scared silly. She checked into getting me a medicine they prescribe for stage fright. "It's not heavy duty," she assured me. "But it will help you calm down."

I prayed for hours the night before that show, and the next day. As the numbers on the digital clock clicked toward the hour of the show, I swallowed the prescribed pill and hoped it would take effect without knocking me off my feet.

That night, Bonita and I took a car to the Kodak Center. Outside, a string of black limos clogged the street as bold and beautiful people like Sharon Stone, Tom Cruise, Denzel Washington, and dozens of other celebrities stepped out to strut over the red carpet. A gaggle of photographers stood behind the velvet ropes, clicking their cameras at every new arrival. I saw Serena Williams stride into the Kodak Theatre, as calm as a Quaker, while reporters stopped other stars for on-the-scene interviews.

The stars and celebrities could keep their red carpets, photographers, and limos. My favorite place was home with my family, tucked away amid the pines and the wildflowers of Mississippi.

Bonita and I had been given passes for the red carpet, but we politely declined. Feeling very much out of our league, we linked arms and scurried along the edge of the red carpet, running into the building like frightened mice.

Once inside, we took our seats. I looked around, searching for familiar faces. I might have actually enjoyed the night if I hadn't been so worried about giving that speech.

When the program began, we settled back in our seats. Faith Hill was supposed to present our award after the midpoint of the program, so I was startled when she walked up to the microphone earlier than I expected. Someone from the side of the stage was hissing at us and gesturing, so Bonita and I stood and stumbled toward the stage.

We gave our speeches, I accepted the huge trophy, and I hoped Brett appreciated everything I was enduring for him.

When it was all over, I collapsed in our hotel room and ordered a pizza. Then I called Brett and told him about the awards ceremony, adding that I couldn't wait to get home.

The stars and celebrities could keep their red carpets, photographers, and limos. My favorite place was home with my family, tucked away amid the pines and the wildflowers of Mississippi.

back-to-back losses

They say it's not unusual to spend more than a year grieving for a lost loved one, particularly if the loss occurred suddenly. Brett's dad passed away in December 2003, so we were still grieving in October 2004 when I received another heart-breaking phone call.

Casey, my twenty-four-year-old brother, had died at our home in Mississippi.

Younger siblings

Casey was born when I was twelve, so I had always felt some-what maternal toward him. I loved changing his diaper when he was first born, and I almost never tired of looking after him. He called me Deedy, and we were extremely close.

Once, when Casey was about two, I remember being invited to spend a week with my aunt and uncle, who lived in another town. Casey cried so hard when I was leaving that

I got in the car with tears in my eyes—he didn't want me to leave, and I didn't want to go with him carrying on like that. But when I came back a week later, he acted as if he'd forgotten who I was. I was brokenhearted for a couple of days while he ignored me. I couldn't believe that my little baby brother would carry on like that, then forget me.

I remember another time when he got really mad at me. He was still a toddler, and I was going to babysit him while my parents went out to eat. As I was holding him at the front door, and he was struggling and trying to get away, an unprintable word slipped out of his mouth. I was *horrified*, not understanding where he'd ever heard such a thing; but he sure knew how to push my buttons.

I have always felt very protective of Casey and Christie, my younger sister. Once, just after Christie was born, I was holding her on my lap when another family member came over and wanted to "hold the new baby." I wasn't about to share. Instead, I scooted out of my seat and took off running out of the house, still clutching baby Christie in my arms. (Boy, did I ever get in trouble for that!) I wasn't about to share "my baby"; but then, what six-year-old likes to share?

Thankfully, I've learned a lot since then.

Tough love

As Casey grew up, he made some bad decisions in his life. Christie and I coddled him to a point, but we kept telling him that he needed to straighten up. We knew we had to take a firm stand with him, and it was incredibly difficult, but we did it because we loved him so much. My experience with Brett had taught me that sometimes tough love is necessary before people will change their ways. After that realization, we chewed Casey out when he made lousy choices, and we stopped giving him money when he asked for it. After we vowed to stop enabling him, we started to see some positive changes.

My mom, Christie, and I began to pray for something that would turn Casey's life around and help him focus on good goals. Not long after that, he introduced us to his girlfriend. A year later, she became pregnant.

We weren't sure we liked the apparent answer to our prayers, but we couldn't deny that the prospect of becoming a father had a positive influence on Casey's life. In early 2004, he got a job working on an offshore oil rig, he began to focus on getting his act together, and he and his girlfriend started saving up to buy a house. When Casey started thinking in terms of *family*, that new focus helped him to stop thinking about drugs and to start planning for the future.

I remember him coming to our home with his girlfriend after a visit to the obstetrician. He had a sonogram picture in his hand and the biggest smile I'd ever seen on his face. "It's a boy," he told me, passing me the photo. "Isn't he beautiful?"

I was so excited for him. Casey was great with children; he'd always been wonderful with my two girls, and I couldn't wait to see him with his own baby.

I was also glad it was a boy. We needed a boy on my mom's side. I wanted a nephew, my mom needed a grandson, and we only had girls on our side.

As the summer ended, we went back to Green Bay for the beginning of football season. One afternoon in September, I stopped at a Walgreens to browse through the card section. A card caught my eye, and I smiled because it reminded me of Casey. I bought the card and addressed it, then added a note, telling Casey that I loved him and was proud of him for making good changes in his life. I dropped the card in the mail.

On October 6, Casey came back to Hattiesburg from working offshore. After going out for lunch with our cousin Robert, he returned to our house to ride ATVs with our cousin Jeremy. Our property is big, more than four hundred acres, and it's nice to ride through some of the wooded areas.

Casey's girlfriend, eight months pregnant, was enjoying the sun out on the deck when she saw someone riding up the road on one of the four-wheel ATVs. The rider was looking at the side of the road and apparently didn't realize that a pile of gravel had been delivered and dumped onto the trail. When the four-wheeler hit the gravel, it flipped in the air and threw the rider off.

Thinking it was Jeremy who had crashed, Casey's girlfriend rushed inside to tell my mother about the accident. But when Mom ran out to investigate, she realized it was Casey, not Jeremy, lying in the grass. He was flat on his back, not moving.

I was at home in Green Bay when Christie called. She had just left work, but had turned around and gone back to the hospital after Josh called to say that Casey was on his way to the emergency room.

"You need to come home," she told me, an edge to her voice. "Casey's been in a bad accident."

I stopped making dinner and blinked in astonishment. A bad accident? Surely someone had made a mistake. Or maybe Casey was just banged up. He was always acting like a wild child, always getting scraped up with one thing or another. This couldn't be *really* bad news, not about Casey. He was only twenty-four and had a baby on the way. Surely nothing serious could happen to him. . . .

But while I was cooking, I told Brett that I probably needed to go home, and asked if he could get me a flight.

While he was doing that, the phone rang again, and again it was Christie. This time, the edge in her voice was replaced by a broken hoarseness. Through anguished sobs, she told me that Casey was gone.

I stood in stunned silence, feeling as if someone had reached into my chest and ripped out my heart. I didn't want to believe it. I just wanted to get home.

I began to think of all the things I'd said or should have said . . . all the memories Casey and I had shared. In that moment, I couldn't help but think of all the times I'd cared for him. Yet now I would never talk to him or see him again. I loved him so much.

Then I thought of the little boy who would be born in four weeks. My little brother would never see his precious baby, the child who had given him purpose and helped him turn his life around. He would never see the baby's first steps or first smile.

I couldn't fathom it. My kitchen suddenly seemed surreal, like it belonged to another place, another time. I wanted to close my eyes, shake my head, and move the hands of the clock back a few hours. Maybe if I started the afternoon over again, I could pretend those two phone calls had never happened.

I stepped outside onto our deck and stood there crying. Thinking about my brother and how much I would miss him was the most heart-wrenching pain I had ever felt in my life. It didn't seem possible that someone so close and so young could simply *go*, leaving me without an opportunity to ever see him again. We had always had such a great relationship—even in the bad times.

Thinking about my brother and how much I would miss him was the most heart-wrenching pain I had ever felt in my life.

I thought about the card I had sent him and realized it would be the last time I was able to tell him how much I loved him. That card would have to be enough. Because he worked offshore and I lived in Green Bay, I hadn't had a chance to hug him in such a long time. That card would have to take the place of my embrace, and I'd have to be comforted by knowing I'd sent it to him—otherwise I'd be torn apart. I couldn't dwell on the fact that I hadn't seen Casey face-to-face or hugged him in such a long time.

I had known darkness before, but those next hours were some of the darkest of my life.

Love must stay tough

Of course, Casey wasn't the first person I'd ever had to handle with "tough love."

By the spring of 1999, when I was pregnant with Breleigh, Brett had fallen back into his habit of partying. He wasn't taking Vicodin, but he was drinking far too much. Furthermore, he realized that he was not able to drink or take any kind of medication without it becoming a problem. He begged me for help, because he didn't want to go back into a rehab program.

Silly me, I thought I could help him.

He would say, "Don't let me drink," and I'd try to stop him whenever he asked me. But then he'd sneak around and do things—and it seemed like the responsibility was somehow on *my* shoulders because I was supposed to be telling him not to do it.

During this time, I was even more depressed than I'd been when Brett was popping pills. At least then I hadn't been pregnant. Now, here I was, carrying the child we had worked so hard to conceive, yet Brett seemed to care more about partying with his friends than being a husband and father. What were we, just a few more trophies for his shelf?

One weekend, Brett was supposed to be camping, but I found out he'd spent the entire night in a bar. When we went to his younger brother Jeff's wedding, Brett told me, "Don't let me drink." I said, "You have to help me, too. You can't hide stuff from me. This has to be a fifty-fifty deal, and you have to do your part."

That night, after the wedding, he looked to me as if he'd been drinking, but I hadn't seen him with a drink in his hand, so I thought he might be okay. As I was sitting at the reception, exhausted and pregnant, a friend told me to go to bed. "I can't," I said. "I can't leave Brett, because I'm supposed to make sure he doesn't drink."

Then Brett came over and said that everyone was going to drive over to Biloxi. He was going along, but he told me I shouldn't worry because he wasn't going to drink.

"Brett," I said, "you shouldn't go. You know what you're going to do, and you know you'll regret it tomorrow."

He tried to argue, but I said, "You asked me to help you, and that's what I'm trying to do. So, no, don't go."

The next thing I knew, Brett and a couple of his friends had vanished. I got my things and went to my friend's house. The next day, when I went back to the Favres' to pick up Brittany, I saw Brett and his friends pulling in at about eight o'clock in the morning. When he saw me, I said, "Is this how you want to live?"

Brittany and I drove back to Hattiesburg that morning, but Brett stayed behind at his parents' house. He didn't call me, and he didn't come home. Instead, he went out again with his friends.

When he finally came home on Monday morning, I had all

TEN WAYS
to stop enabling the addict in your life

WHAT IS LOVE? THE BIBLE TELLS US:

> *Love is patient and kind. Love is not jealous or boastful or*
> *proud or rude. It does not demand its own way. It is not*
> *irritable, and it keeps no record of being wronged. It does not*
> *rejoice about injustice but rejoices whenever the truth wins out.*
> *Love never gives up, never loses faith, is always hopeful, and*
> *endures through every circumstance.*[1]

Do you see anything in that passage about love being willing to lie? That love covers up? That love helps the loved one to destroy himself?

When I moved to Green Bay, I loved Brett, and I wanted to spend the rest of my life with him. But when I began to realize how the drug addiction had changed him, I saw that what we had wasn't love. If I gave in to his demands, if I didn't hold him accountable for the things he was doing, I wasn't loving him; I was only helping him on a path to self-destruction.

Recently I read something profound:

Helping is doing something that someone else is not capable of doing himself.

Enabling is doing something that someone else could and should be doing himself.[2]

You help feed a child or invalid who cannot feed himself. You enable the alcoholic or drug abuser when you force him to eat for his health's sake.

If your loved one is going to recover from whatever unhealthy addiction has captured his heart, mind, and body, you must stop enabling certain behaviors.

The following list is not inclusive, but here are some things to guide you as you seek to exercise real love.

1. Do not lie for the addict under any circumstance. Do not call in sick for him, do not "fudge" the truth or practice any sort of deception on his behalf. Lying is not a kindness.

2. Do not accept blame for your loved one's destructive behavior. Do not make excuses for his sloppy or nonexistent work. Do not believe that his problem will go away on its own. It won't.

3. Do not be afraid to talk about your loved one's drinking/drug use/compulsive spending, or other unwise behavior.

4. Do not bail him out of jail or pay his legal fees.

5. Do not pay his bills.

6. Do not loan him money. Do not bribe him with something desirable if he'll stop drinking or go to treatment.

7. Do not drink or use drugs with him. Do not engage in the destructive behavior with your loved one. Misery loves company, so don't make him comfortable in his problem.

8. Regardless of how many chances you've given in the past, do not give any more. Draw a line and do not accept any more excuses. If you've made a threat ("I'll kick you out . . ."), you must follow through.

9. Do not finish a job or project that your loved one should have finished himself. Do not clean up after him.

10. Do not forget to take care of yourself.

You cannot force your loved one to change, but you can change your own behavior. Stop enabling him, and start practicing tough love. ❧

his belongings packed and waiting in the courtyard of the house. I'd become so desperate that I had called a divorce attorney.

Don't get me wrong—I know divorce is a big deal, and it wasn't how I wanted my marriage to end up. But my thinking was so confused, and my heart so broken, that I had begun to wonder if I wouldn't be hurting my children more by remaining in a marriage where I seemed to be an afterthought rather than a partner. I didn't want a separation or divorce; I wanted a happy home. But with every day that passed, my goal seemed more and more out of reach. It felt like things were never going to change, and I couldn't believe all the junk I was having to endure.

Talk about tough love. Delivering that ultimatum broke my heart, but I knew that Brett's lifestyle wasn't good for me, for our children, or for him.

He came into the house and begged me to let him stay, but I was firm. "If you're not going to quit drinking, you can leave," I told him. "I'm not going down that road again; I'm done. I've already spoken to an attorney."

"I'm sorry," Brett said. "I'll never do it again."

"I don't care," I answered. "Don't whine to me about being sorry. I tried to help you, but I can't. You're going to have to do this on your own."

The attorney called while Brett was begging me to reconsider, and Brett heard me tell her I was ready to file; that I was done and there was no changing my mind.

I think Brett was shocked. Then, as the Lord would have it, the phone rang again. It was Pam Johnston, the friend who'd been my matron of honor and wedding cake baker, calling for the first time in months. As soon as I heard her voice, I burst into tears. She knew about our situation, and more than once she'd prayed with me to help me get through a bad time.

So there I was, bawling on the phone, telling her that I was finished with my marriage—that I'd had it. Brett was in the next room, hearing every word, and he knew this time I absolutely meant it.

When I hung up, I told Brett that if he didn't get out of my house, I would call 9-1-1. I called his agent, and Bus came to pick him up. Brett told Bus to take him to the airport, because he was going to check himself into rehab again.

I listened, my feelings numb. At that point, I honestly wanted nothing more to do with Brett Favre. Later, when counselors said we needed to have some counseling sessions together, I wasn't sure I was ready to do that. My heart was still aching and raw.

But I did. And Brett realized that if he wanted a life with me and the children, he couldn't drink again. He gave it up completely, and it's been eight years since he's had a drink.

Was tough love worth the pain? Absolutely. I've learned that sometimes people have to hit rock bottom before they realize that something's not right. Sometimes you have to do something to shake them up. You have to let them hit bottom. I used to think that I had to stay and try to help Brett, but I was taking mental abuse and he didn't even realize it.

Since Brett stopped drinking, our lifestyle has changed, and the quality of our life together has changed as well. We're not about partying; we're about making a home for our daughters and doing what we can for others.

Because I saw how "tough love" helped Brett, I was sure it would help Casey, too. And it did . . . it changed his life.

So why did God take Casey just when he was beginning to grow up? I couldn't help but wonder.

Saying good-bye

Arriving in Mississippi for Casey's funeral was hard. We had to make preparations for his burial, and I had to choose the coffin. My mom and dad were there, as well as Christie and her husband, but we were all so devastated. Somehow, we made all the arrangements together and got through the process.

We had Casey's funeral at the Baptist church he used to attend with my grandfather. He'd always been close to Grandpa. During the viewing, I walked down to the front of the church and studied my brother in his casket, looking for all the world like he was only asleep. In a way, I suppose that's what death is, isn't it? A rest for these tired earthly bodies until the Lord resurrects them.

I reached for Casey's hand and rubbed a spot that still felt soft. I never wanted to let go.

Christie walked up to my side and stood for a moment—then she made a crack about Casey's hair. He usually wore a hat, so if he was watching from heaven, he was probably rolling his eyes at the thought of so many people seeing his hair combed for a change.

"Do you remember," I asked, "how he was always blaming Aunt Geraldine for his tendency to put on weight?"

When Casey was young, my mom's older sister watched him for a while while my mom was at work, and she fed him nonstop. It seemed like every hour she'd ask, "Want something to eat?" After that, every time his weight fluctu-ated and he put on a few pounds, he'd tell Mom, "I wouldn't have this problem if you hadn't let Aunt Geraldine feed me all the time."

In that moment, I began to understand what people mean when they say they are "homesick for heaven."

Christie smiled at the memory. "At least now with his new body, he'll never have to worry about gaining weight."

Casey had been gone for only a few hours, but already we

were longing to see him again. In that moment, I began to understand what people mean when they say they are "homesick for heaven."

We talked about the baby. I couldn't imagine never being able to see Casey with his son. I know he would have been a phenomenal dad.

We talked about the memories—about how I had babied him, and the time he let the unprintable word rip when he threw a temper tantrum.

And then we said good-bye.

When baby Casey was born a month later, Christie and I snuggled him and knew that we'd been blessed with a sweet reminder of our beloved brother. Even now, he will smile or make a face and I'll melt right where I'm standing.

God has his reasons, but he also has his blessings. One of them is to know that my brother lives on in his son. Another is to know that heaven awaits, and I will be reunited with so many loved ones who have gone there before me.

suddenly sidelined

Job, you may recall, endured a second test after the deaths of his children and the loss of his livestock. Satan went back to the throne room of heaven, and God said:

> "Have you noticed my servant Job? He is the finest man in all the earth. He is blameless—a man of complete integrity. He fears God and stays away from evil. And he has maintained his integrity, even though you urged me to harm him without cause."
>
> Satan replied to the LORD, "Skin for skin! A man will give up everything he has to save his life. But reach out and take away his health, and he will surely curse you to your face!"
>
> "All right, do with him as you please," the LORD said to Satan. "But spare his life." So Satan left the LORD's presence, and he struck Job with terrible boils from head to foot.[1]

Finding a lump

We buried my brother on Saturday, October 9, 2004. The next day, I flew back to Green Bay. (The Packers had a Monday night game, in which they would be defeated by the Tennessee Titans, 48–27.)

It was not a good week for any of us.

Two months earlier, during a regular breast self-exam, I had found a small lump between my right armpit and my

HOW TO
conduct a breast self-exam

If there is one thing you take away from this book, I hope it's this: breast self-exams are important. It's crucial for you to know your body. If you do a self-exam every month, you'll get to know your body, and you'll realize when there are changes. That's how early detection works—you stumble upon a lump that has just popped up.

Early detection is definitely the key to beating cancer. You don't want to find a lump that has been growing for two years, but that's what can happen if you don't do regular self-exams. When I went to the doctor about my lump, I was able to tell him exactly when it appeared, because it was obvious one month and hadn't been obvious the month before.

A thorough breast self-exam involves two parts: looking and feeling.

To visually examine your breasts, stand in front of a wide mirror with your shirt and bra removed. You are going to examine the shape and size of your breasts first—become familiar with what is normal for you so you will be able to notice any changes. Don't be alarmed if one of your breasts is larger than the other. You want to notice changes in what is normal for *you*.

Examine your breasts with your arms raised, then lowered. Next, press down on your hips with your hands and lean forward, breast. I thought it was odd, but I didn't worry about it for several reasons—first, I had no family history of breast cancer. Second, the lump was perfectly round, and I'd recently read a magazine article that said most cancers are jagged or irregular in shape. Finally, I was only thirty-five, and I exercised regularly and ate well. I thought of myself as strong and healthy.

A couple days later, I had Christie, who's a nurse practitioner, assess the lump. She wasn't alarmed either, though she did make me promise to get it checked out at my next

looking for any signs of dimpling in the skin. Notice the color and texture of your skin—has it changed since last month?

Next, fold a bath towel and lie on the bed, placing the folded towel beneath your right shoulder. Extend your right arm over your head and use your left hand to probe your right breast. Be sure to examine the entire area from your collarbone to what would be the bottom of your bra, and from your armpit to your breastbone. Use the pads of your fingers and make small circles, probing for lumps with light, then medium, then deep pressure. Cover the entire breast, moving up and down, until you've probed every inch. You are searching for a firm lump or a thickening that feels different from the other breast tissue. Repeat this procedure for your left breast, moving the towel from your right to your left shoulder.

If you find a lump or thickening, see your doctor as soon as possible. The vast majority of breast lumps are *not* cancerous—they may be fluid-filled cysts or fibrous tissue. But if you do have a growth of abnormal cells, early detection and prompt treatment will give you the best odds of completely defeating cancer.

We have included a self-exam chart in the back of the book. I strongly encourage you to cut it out and hang it in your bathroom to serve as a visual reminder to check your breasts every month. &

doctor's appointment. "It might be a cyst," she said. "Some women notice them around the time of their cycles, but they're harmless."

When I first found the lump, it felt like a perfect little BB. By the time I went for my annual gynecological appointment in October, four days after returning from Casey's funeral, I could tell the lump had grown to the size of a marble. I still wasn't alarmed, but my doctor thought we should check it out. Thinking it might be a cyst, he tried to aspirate it, but he couldn't get any fluid out of the mass. Though insisting he wasn't worried, he sent me to see Dr. Lyle Henry at Columbia St. Mary's Hospital in Milwaukee. I learned that Columbia St. Mary's is affiliated with the Van Dyke Haebler Center, a diagnostic breast cancer facility that offers digital mammography, ultrasound, and all the latest technology, all under one roof.

If I ruled the world, I would see that every city or region had a freestanding breast cancer center. The wonderful Van Dyke Haebler Center has state-of-the-art equipment, including MRIs and ultrasound machines. Because everything is on-site, a patient can have a consultation, mammogram, ultrasound, and even a biopsy, in the course of one day.

A woman who finds a lump doesn't want to wait two weeks or more to know whether she has cancer. Some women who discover they do have cancer have to wait more than a month to schedule the surgery that could save their lives. That's horrible. That's why I wish every region could have its own center—so women can get results quickly and meet the teams who will assist them in getting better.

As my friend Sue Romppanen and I drove to Milwaukee for my appointment, I kept telling myself that I didn't have cancer. Still, I wanted to remove all doubt about that troublesome cyst.

Better safe than sorry, right?

The first person I met at the Van Dyke Haebler Center was Deb Theine, a slender, dark-haired nurse, who would be escorting me through each station at the cancer center, including the mammography area, the ultrasound room, and the radiology lab.

Our first stop was to meet Dr. Henry, and I liked him immediately. He's bald, with a quick sense of humor and eyes that nearly disappear into laugh lines when he smiles. Best of all, he smiles *a lot*. I was encouraged to see that he could find humor in what was beginning to feel like a grim situation. I remember asking him at one point whether my hair would fall out if I had to have chemotherapy. (Brett's aunt had gone through chemo and hadn't lost her hair.) Dr. Henry smiled, rubbed the top of his head, and said, "Maybe, but I don't feel sorry for you, because your hair will grow back. Mine won't."

After Dr. Henry and I exchanged initial greetings, he and Deb took me to meet the radiologist, the plastic surgeon, the radiation oncologist, and everyone else who might be on my cancer-fighting team. They all explained what their roles would be if I needed them.

I was so impressed when Dr. Henry greeted every person we met by name. "We're going to take good care of you," he assured me, and I believed him. "We'll start with a mammogram, then take you through the stations until we know exactly what's going on."

I left Sue in the waiting area and went to a changing area to put on the elbow-length cape Deb gave me. A moment later, she called me into the darkened room where the mammography machine awaited. Pam Piel, the bright and cheerful technician, kept up a running stream of conversation as she adjusted my shoulders, my arms, and my breast to get the best possible X-rays. I'd heard dozens of jokes about mammograms and steamrollers—about how both are likely to squeeze you as flat as a frog on a four-lane highway—but the experience wasn't bad. Believe me, childbirth is worse.

After my mammogram—my first—the radiologist came in with my films and said I'd been cleared to go to ultrasound. By using ultrasound, they would be able to see exactly what they were doing as they tried to aspirate the lump.

I tried not to be nervous as I lay on the table in the darkened room. They had numbed my breast, so all I felt was a little pressure at my side when the needle pierced the skin and probed the lump. In a moment, it was all over and a technician took the sample away.

I sat up, arranged the folds of my cape around me, and wished I'd brought something to read. The waiting was tedious, but I knew this was nothing compared to what other women endure. At least this cancer center had all the tools in one location.

When Dr. Patrick McWey, my radiologist, returned a few moments later, he said we needed to do a biopsy.

> *When Dr. Patrick McWey, my radiologist, returned a few moments later, he said we needed to do a biopsy. I felt my heart pound a double beat as I met his concerned gaze. "Why?"*

I felt my heart pound a double beat as I met his concerned gaze. "Why?"

"Well, there were some cells, some abnormal cells."

"Will that . . . will the biopsy tell you if I have cancer?"

He gave me a careful smile. "The material has to sit in a solution overnight, but we'll call you tomorrow."

"Will you give me the results over the phone?" I was dreading the long drive back to Milwaukee.

He nodded. "I will."

Biopsy

Fortunately, improvements in medical technology have made breast biopsies easier for patients as well as doctors.

The type I had is called a *core needle* biopsy. The procedure is similar to the fine needle aspiration they did with the ultrasound, but it's a little more involved. I was taken to a room and asked to lie on a table. Then I was given a local anesthetic to numb the area around my breast. The surgical team surrounded me, their eyes warm and caring above their surgical masks.

From the corner of my eye, I saw the needle in the surgeon's gloved hand—this was a lot larger than the needle used to obtain the first sample of cells.

I turned my head. I'm not as queasy around needles as Brett is, but I figured there was no sense in watching them use my breast as a pincushion, either.

As he worked, Dr. McWey explained what he was doing. He would insert the needle three to six times, until he was sure he had enough tissue samples. I heard a slight clicking sound and felt a subtle pressure at my side, but nothing painful. The nurse watched and occasionally handed the doctor a fresh slide. The procedure was finished much faster than I had expected.

A core needle biopsy, I learned, is a better analysis tool than fine needle aspiration because the doctor removes actual tissue instead of just a few random cells. The only time the procedure is not used is if the lump is very small or very hard.[2]

Other types of biopsy are *vacuum-assisted,* in which a vacuum-like device is used to withdraw breast tissue; *large core* biopsy, which uses a tube and a cutting device to remove the lump in one piece; and *open excisional,* the most involved type of biopsy, in which a small incision is made as close to the lump as possible, the surgeon shaves off a piece of tissue (if the lump is small, he might remove it entirely), and then sutures the incision. Even this surgery is not terribly involved, and the incision usually heals in about a month.[3]

Of course, every woman's case is different, so if you find yourself in my situation, I encourage you to get at least two opinions, ask your doctors about the different options, and then trust their recommendation for the best way to proceed.

The binder

After the biopsy, Deb Theine waited for me to get dressed, and then she led Sue and me into a softly lit conference room. As I sat at a table, Deb took the chair beside me and slid a thick binder in my direction. Sue sat nearby and pulled out a notebook and a pen.

I looked at the title page and swallowed hard. The binder was filled with information about breast cancer.

I looked up and caught Deb's eye. "Do . . . do you think I have cancer?"

"I don't know," Deb said, her voice level. "But it's best to be prepared."

As she opened the binder and began to explain various options and treatments, I realized why she was giving me this information now. If tomorrow I learned that I had cancer, I'd be in such shock that I probably wouldn't retain anything but that one dreadful fact. On the other hand, if tomorrow I learned that all I had was a stubborn cyst, at least I'd be better educated.

Education is so important; it is a huge factor in cancer treatment. In the old days, most breast cancer patients were treated with a mastectomy, period. Now there are options, and as I learned that day, you don't automatically have to lose your breasts.

I listened to Deb, nodding and smiling while Sue took frantic notes.

"I don't believe I have cancer," I said several times. "After all, I'm healthy. And I'm only thirty-five."

I'm sure that Deb has heard every possible response from women as they wait for their results. She continued her

FIVE WAYS
to remember when it's time for your BSE

The number one reason why women fail to do their monthly breast self-exams? They forget. Prevailing wisdom says you should do your self-check at the end of your menstrual cycle each month, but because that's a gradual event, too many women forget. And what about our post-menopausal friends? Here are five suggestions from my co-author, Angela Hunt, to help you remember.

1. Celebrate your birthday every month. If you were born on the fourteenth, remember to thank God for another month of life on the fourteenth of every month . . . and do your BSE so you'll celebrate many more birthday months.

2. Think of your BSE as a "mortgage" for good health. Right after writing out your mortgage or rent payment, do your BSE.

3. Have a dog? If you give your dog a monthly heartworm pill, use those little heart-shaped calendar stickers to also remind you that it's time for your BSE.

4. Program your computer calendar to remind you when it's time for your BSE. Download the audio file to "Bend Me, Shape Me," by The American Breed, and let it play as an alarm!

5. What's shiny and round and reminds us of romance? The moon, of course. Whenever you look up into the night sky and see a full moon, let it remind you to conduct your monthly breast self-exam. You'll be glad you did. ॐ

explanations in a calm and professional manner, educating me about breast cancer and telling me what to expect if my biopsy revealed malignant cells. She was completely, blessedly neutral—I didn't get the feeling I had cancer, but neither did she give me false assurance.

Before the day ended, I had talked to a radiation oncologist, a plastic surgeon, and an entire cancer treatment team. Whenever I began to feel a little nervous and ask, "Do you think I might have—," someone always replied, "We certainly hope not."

Brett called my cell phone every hour, wanting to know if I knew anything. When he called around three or four in the afternoon, I told him they were doing the biopsy, but I was sure it'd be fine, no big deal. I could tell he was concerned that I was spending all day at the cancer clinic. He'd been thinking I'd be in and out in an hour or two.

Sue and I drove back to Green Bay and tried to behave as if the day had been completely ordinary. I made dinner, loaded the dishwasher, watched a little television, and went to bed. I kept telling myself that I had just lost my brother a few days ago, so there was no way I would have cancer, too. The odds were simply too great.

Just a cyst. That's surely all I had. Just a stubborn cyst.

Diagnosis

The next morning, Brett went to work, Breleigh went to school, and I went to exercise. After I showered and dressed, I didn't want to be nervously pacing around the house and waiting for the doctor's call, so I drove to my friend Toni's house and kept my cell phone within reach.

Every time the phone rang, my heart lurched in my chest. But every time the phone rang that morning, it was Brett on the other end of the line. No matter how many times I told him I didn't expect to hear anything until after noon, he kept calling. Finally, I told him to hang up and go run some laps or something. "Study your playbook, sign some autographs, throw a few footballs. Just don't call me again until after twelve-thirty."

At five minutes past twelve, my phone rang again. I answered, half-expecting to hear Brett's voice again, but Dr. Henry was on the line.

I heard my answer in his first word: "Dear . . ."

No way.

"The biopsy shows that you do, in fact, have breast cancer."

A trembling rose from somewhere in the marrow of my bones, chilling my blood and shivering my skin. I felt as if I were standing naked in twenty-degree weather.

Cancer.

My mind filled with images of bald women—thin-armed, pale-faced mothers in hospital beds with their husbands and children gathered around.

A buzzing filled my ears, a sound so loud I could barely hear the man on the other end of the line.

A trembling rose from somewhere in the marrow of my bones, chilling my blood and shivering my skin. I felt as if I were standing naked in twenty-degree weather.

I had to force myself to concentrate on the phone against my ear.

"We'll get you an appointment for tomorrow," Dr. Henry was saying. "What time can you get here?"

I said I would be there first thing in the morning. I wanted to get this over with ASAP.

"Fine. Any questions?"

I blinked, unable to find the words to answer him. What

could I say? Deb Theine had explained all the facts, but none of them had applied to me, because yesterday I didn't have cancer.

At least I didn't *know* I did. But hearing Dr. Henry's voice brought the truth home with stunning force.

I had a loving husband, two daughters, a wonderful life.

And breast cancer.

Unavoidable. True. Deadly.

Brett didn't wait until twelve-thirty. I had barely disconnected the doctor's call when my phone rang again. Without even saying hello, Brett asked, "Did you hear anything?"

When I didn't—couldn't—answer, he exhaled a jagged breath. "Oh, God."

His spontaneous prayer would have to suffice; I was too numb to pray.

tough calls

When Brett called and realized the awful truth, he told me he was coming straight home. Because I was still at Toni's, I realized I'd have to go to the house and meet him there.

Before leaving, though, I went to Toni's computer and looked for pictures of mastectomies on the Internet. I wanted to see photographs of the worst I could expect. I knew I could lose my breast. If I had to face that reality, I wanted to be prepared.

The thought of losing my breast was terrifying, but I would do it if that's what it took to get the cancer out of my body.

When I met Brett at the house, I discovered that my usually confident husband had gone pale. I'd never seen him at such a loss for words—he didn't know what to say or how to act. In retrospect, I think he was more in shock than I was.

Brett later told a reporter from *USA Today* about my diagnosis. "All I know is that when you hear *cancer*, it sounds like a death sentence. It's not, and it's treatable, but I still didn't want my wife to have it. I was worried sick for her safety. And for our girls, who could lose their mom and would run the risk of having it. . . . Nothing positive went through my mind for a while."[1]

As Brett and I held each other, all kinds of thoughts flew through my brain. I shivered, feeling cold and nervous and tense, all at the same time. I thought of my girls and wondered how I was supposed to give them this awful news.

We hugged for a long time and assured each other that everything was going to be all right. We'd faced tough times before, hadn't we?

When I talked to my mother, I assured her I was going to be fine. The doctors had told me they had every hope for my full recovery, so I focused on relaying that information to my loved ones. I went into "comforter mode," while Brett attacked the breast cancer binder I'd brought home from the doctor's office like it was the opposing team's playbook.

> *I went into "comforter mode," while Brett attacked the breast cancer binder I'd brought home from the doctor's office like it was the opposing team's playbook.*

I have to give him credit, because he really studied it. He began to look things up and kept telling me what the experts said about various treatment options. I wasn't really ready to hear him, though, because part of me was still in denial. A voice in the back of my mind kept insisting that everything would go away. If the cancer didn't disappear on its own, I would have the surgery, have the lump cut out, and everything would be fine.

I didn't even want to call the lump by its rightful name: *malignant tumor*. To me, it was still a marble-size lump, a knot of tissue that had somehow grown in my body by mistake.

I still had to tell my daughters about the upcoming surgery. Brittany was in Mississippi with my sister, so I told her over the phone, but I made sure Christie was right there when I called. I was nonchalant as I described the surgery and treatment, and played everything down as much as I could. "I don't want you to worry," I said, "but I've been diagnosed with breast cancer. We believe we caught it really early, and I'm going to be fine. I'm going to go through all the steps and do whatever I have to in order to get well."

Brittany was only fifteen, so I didn't want to burden her with my news. She was a little sad when I told her, but she's strong and she remained positive. She kept encouraging me and saying that I'd be fine, and I took heart from her attitude. I'm sure any daughter would be a little upset to hear that her mom has cancer, but Brittany's pretty smart. She was able to do a little research, and she learned that breast cancer is one of the most treatable cancers—and we had caught mine in the early stages. Plus, she was staying with Christie, and I knew my sister could answer any of Britt's medical questions. She showed a lot of strength and courage when I gave her the news, and now that she realizes that she has a family history of breast cancer, breast self-exams will always be important to her.

Telling five-year-old Breleigh was a bit more complicated. The cancer center had given me a little book called *My Mom Has Cancer,* so I brought it home so we could read it together. I knew that I needed to radiate strength and calm when I talked to her.

We sat on the sofa in the den with some of her favorite books, and then I introduced the new book. I just wanted to make sure she was as comforted as she could be. Five-year-olds question everything, and Breleigh was no exception. She was filled with questions. I told her I would be sick for a while and that I would lose my hair, but it would grow back.

"Why?" she asked. "Why does your hair have to fall out?"

I should have expected that Breleigh's biggest fear would center on something tangible: the possibility that I might lose my hair.

I've always had long hair, except for the time I cut my hair for Locks of Love, the nonprofit organization that collects

HOW TO
talk to your kids about breast cancer

Ordinarily, we would like to spare our children anything that might cause them to feel worried or afraid, but experts tell us it's far better to be honest when breast cancer strikes a family. So gather your children around and tell them the truth, keeping the following points in mind:

- Children will sense that something is wrong, so don't deny the truth. Tell them you have cancer, you're being treated, and you're going to do everything possible to get well. If you are optimistic, they will be too.

- Use the words *breast cancer.* Otherwise they may imagine that you have some sort of contagious disease or that your entire body is sick. Let them know it's okay to hug and kiss you.

- Make sure that younger children understand that cancer is no one's fault. Younger children tend to blame themselves when something goes wrong in a family, so let them know that cancer is not the result of anything anyone has done.

- Prepare them for the future. Describe your treatment in terms your children can understand. Let them know about your surgery, chemotherapy, and/or radiation. Say, "I might lose my hair, but it will grow back. And I might be tired and grumpy for a while, but those feelings will pass, too."

- Encourage your children to ask questions. Tell them that you'll try to find the answer for any question you can't donated hair and makes wigs for financially disadvantaged children suffering from long-term medical hair loss. Even then, Breleigh didn't like seeing me with short hair. She's always been attached to my hair; she used to fall asleep on my pillow with a handful of my hair pressed against her cheek.

I told Breleigh that I had to take medicine that would get rid

answer. Far better to encourage a spirit of openness than to have your child worrying in secret.

- Reassure your children that they will be cared for in the months ahead. Children often worry about what might happen to them if their primary caretaker is disabled, so let your children know that Dad, Grandma, Aunt Sue, or the regular babysitter will be around to help take care of things.

- Check out available resources. Ask around at your cancer center or hospital to see if there are support groups for children whose parents are battling cancer, especially if your children seem depressed or their schoolwork begins to suffer.

- Cling to the ordinary. Help keep your family routine as normal as possible. Try to schedule your treatments while your children are in school; do your best to keep life flowing in a normal pattern.

- Display optimism and faith. Children often learn what is seen and not heard, so your optimistic attitude will do more to encourage your children than a dozen pep talks.

- Don't neglect your spiritual life. Prayer and meditating on Bible verses will bolster your spirit, which will also encourage your children. ❧

of the cancer, and the medicine would be what made my hair fall out. The little book was very helpful, because it explained

I should have expected that Breleigh's biggest fear would center on something tangible: the possibility that I might lose my hair.

what I would be going through and the changes she might actually see. She was too young to understand much about cancer, so we focused on

the things she would be seeing in the weeks ahead. The hair loss was a mystery to her, and worrisome.

But hair loss, I figured, was a small price to pay for my life.

Moving ahead

The next morning, I drove back to Milwaukee to meet with Dr. Henry and his team. Invasive breast cancers are categorized as stage I, II, III, or IV. Stages I and II are considered "early stage" and usually refer to small tumors that have not spread. Dr. Henry felt that mine was a stage II, which would require a lumpectomy (not a mastectomy) and chemo, but because premenopausal women tend to have more faster-growing cancers, he said I would need to be treated aggressively, even though the cancer had been caught at an early stage. The doctors couldn't tell me anything more until after they'd examined the tumor and the lymph nodes, so Dr. Henry recommended that I have the surgery as soon as possible.

Meanwhile, Brett was cornering every doctor he knew in Green Bay and asking, "What would you do if this were your wife?" They all gave him the same answer: "I'd take her to Sloan-Kettering in New York."

We had friends who owned a condo in New York, and they offered to let us use their home. My mom came up to stay with Breleigh, and by Monday night Brett, Christie, Sue, and I were on our way to New York.

On Tuesday morning, we walked into Memorial Sloan-Kettering Cancer Center to get an official second opinion. My doctor at Sloan-Kettering, Dr. Alexandria Heerdt, agreed with Dr. Henry that my best option would be a lumpectomy followed by chemotherapy. She couldn't say how intense the chemo would be until after an examination of the edges of the tumor and a sentinel node biopsy.

TEN QUESTIONS *every woman should ask her doctor after a breast cancer diagnosis*

1. What type of tumor do I have? What does "invasive" mean?

2. What is an "early stage" breast cancer?

3. With a cancer like mine, what are the survival rates for each type of treatment?

4. Why would a woman choose to have a mastectomy if the survival rate is the same with a lumpectomy?

5. I have a family history of breast cancer. Should my treatment be more aggressive?

6. Does the type of surgery I choose affect whether or not I should have chemotherapy?

7. For my type of cancer and my recommended treatment, what are the odds of cancer recurring?

8. Will my skin be affected by the radiation?

9. If I choose a mastectomy, can I have reconstructive surgery at the same time?

10. Should I get a second opinion?

"If you want to stay here," Dr. Heerdt said, "we can prob-ably do the lumpectomy on Friday." I knew that if I went back to Green Bay, I'd have to wait a week or two because Dr. Henry was going on vacation.

I looked at Brett, who squeezed my hand and said, "I think you should just do it."

I told Dr. Heerdt to sign me up for Friday.

Brett had to fly back to Green Bay because he had prac-tice on Wednesday, so Sue and Christie stayed with me in New York. Despite the fact I had a couple of pre-surgical appointments, we had a few days to enjoy the city and—I hoped—take our minds off of what lay ahead. We shopped, ate in some fabulous restaurants, and went to see *Hairspray* on Broadway. After a fun girls' night out, we went back to the hotel to watch the Yankees and the Red Sox in the American League Championship Series on TV.

It was a great series, and because we were in New York, we felt a personal connection. When the Red Sox beat the Yankees in a miraculous comeback that stunned baseball fans around the nation, we stayed up late to watch the games, and it was so exciting that I was almost able to forget the surgery awaiting me on Friday.

The night before the surgery, I prayed for the doctor, for the surgery, and for my attitude—I wanted to be strong and positive. I kept thinking about my husband and my girls, and I couldn't forget that even having general anesthesia was a calculated risk.

I prayed that everything would come out all right.

Lumpectomy

The morning before the surgery, I called Brett. He assured me that everything would be fine and told me he loved me.

"Whatever happens," he said, "I'll be here, and I'm really positive they're going to remove all the cancer. So don't you worry about anything; just be strong and get through it."

"Say a prayer for me," I told him, "and I love you."

Christie and Sue were with me before the attendants took me into the operating room. I spoke to my doctor before they gave me the anesthetic. I believed I was in good hands, and it was comforting to know that Christie and Sue were with me.

I was grateful that my tumor was not so large or my cancer so advanced that I'd require a mastectomy. Having the lumpectomy would allow me to keep my breast, with only a small scar to show for the experience.

In a lumpectomy, the surgeon makes a small incision over or near the tumor and cuts the lump out along with a margin of at least one centimeter (approximately one-half inch) of surrounding breast tissue.[2] I was fortunate because the surgery would not leave me at all disfigured. Clear fluid usually fills the cavity after the lump is removed and gradually the body replaces the fluid with scar tissue. The area would be tender for a while, but infection and bleeding are rare.

I was told that the pathologist would examine my tumor while I was still in the operating room, and that they would ascertain during the surgery whether the cancer had spread. The surgeon would remove two or three lymph nodes and examine them to see if they were free of cancer cells. If they were, the surgeon would stop there. But if they discovered cancer cells in those first lymph nodes, the surgeon would remove additional nodes until she found one that was cancer free.

A sentinel node biopsy, I learned, is a way of pinpointing the first few lymph nodes into which a tumor drains. Rather than remove nodes unnecessarily, doctors remove only those nodes that are most likely to contain cancer cells. If a node is positive for cancer, other nearby lymph nodes may be positive as well. If it is negative, it is highly likely that all the surrounding nodes are also negative.

To locate the sentinel nodes, either a radioactive tracer, blue dye, or both are injected into the area around the tumor before it is removed. The tracer travels the same path to the lymph nodes that cancer cells would take, making it possible for the surgeon to determine the one or two nodes most likely to test positive for malignant cells.[3]

"If we find cancer in the nodes," Dr. Heerdt told me, "you'll probably wake up with a drain in your arm to remove excess fluid that would accumulate and cause swelling."

When I woke up in the recovery room, my first words were, "Do I have a drain?" I didn't. The surgeons had removed three lymph nodes, and they were all clean. The margins around my tumor were clean, too, so the surgical team was sure they had gotten all the cancer. But just in case a rogue cancer cell had avoided detection, the doctors wanted to be aggressive with my treatment.

I'd always been a tomboy and an athlete. How tough could chemo be?

After returning to Green Bay, I learned that I would be treated with four doses of the Cytoxan and Adriamycin "chemo cocktail"—one treatment every two weeks, followed by six weeks of radiation. I was ready to meet cancer head-on, and I was certain I could remain strong in the face of whatever came my way.

After all, I'd always been a tomboy and an athlete. How tough could chemo be?

playing with pain

As I look back on the time of my diagnosis and surgery, I realize that I was a little numb through the entire experience. I was still going through the grieving process over my brother's death, so maybe I wasn't as upset as someone else would be. I was shocked, but not devastated. Compared to the finality of sudden death, a small case of breast cancer didn't seem terribly overwhelming.

The day after my surgery in New York, I flew home to Green Bay and spent two weeks recovering. On November 22, Brett went with me for my first chemo treatment.

That initial encounter is as much a mental battle as a physical one. *Chemotherapy* sounds so foreign; it's not a word I had ever associated with myself. But if I was going to fight cancer and do everything I could to ensure my long-term survival, chemo and I were going to have to become friends. I braced myself, took Brett's hand, and strode into the clinic.

How chemo works

Chemotherapy is the administration of drugs that work throughout your body to kill cancer cells that may have spread. One of my first questions was, how do the drugs differentiate between healthy cells and cancer cells?

Your body's normal cells grow and divide in a controlled, organized fashion. Cancer cells, on the other hand, multiply and divide without rhyme or reason. They are rapidly dividing cells. Chemotherapy stops the growth and multiplication of rapidly dividing cells, an act that effectively "kills" the cancer. It may kill other rapidly dividing cells in your body, too, but that's part of the price you pay to wipe out the cancer. Unfortunately, science has not yet advanced to the point where the drugs can differentiate between a "good" rapidly dividing cell and a "bad" one.

The cells in your blood, mouth, nose, intestinal tract, vagina, nails, and hair are also undergoing constant, rapid division.[1] The chemo drugs will affect them as well, but in time your body can repair the damage done to these healthy cells. Your hair will grow back, your nails will grow strong again, and your stomach will settle. Some systems in your body may require more time to recover, but the human body does an amazing job of putting itself back together.

When used as systemic therapy right after surgery, chemo has another advantage—it's being used in the right place at the right time. Let's say that a cancer cell or two *does* break away from the tumor and escape detection. On their own, the freewheeling cancer cells have lots of nutrients and oxygen, so they're free to grow and divide at a quick rate. However, because the chemo targets and kills rapidly dividing cells, the weeks after surgery are the perfect time for treatment.[2]

First-round knockdown

I was scheduled to receive my treatments at St. Vincent Hospital in Green Bay. My appointment wasn't until 5:00 p.m., so I tried to pass the day with normal activities—I got up, took Breleigh to school, and did my workout. I didn't worry about cooking dinner for a change, because my Bible study group had decided to provide meals for us for several days. Someone was scheduled to have dinner waiting for us when we got home.

Once Brett and I had been ushered into a private room on the second floor, a nurse came in to talk to us about the two drugs I'd be receiving—Cytoxan and Adriamycin, known as the "red devil" because of its fiery color.

The nurse told me everything I needed to know—what to do if I got sick, how to avoid nausea by eating several light meals instead of three large ones, and how to avoid dehydration by sipping water and keeping a cup of shaved ice on hand. She gave me Compazine pills for nausea, and steroids to encourage my appetite.

The Cytoxan made my nose burn, like the feeling you sometimes get when you dive underwater. But if you chew on a piece of candy, it lessens the unpleasant sensation.

The nurse told me to drink flat Coke if I felt nauseated, but the very thought of it made me queasy. She said I could take my chemo treatments through a vein, a port, or a PICC line (a peripherally inserted central catheter), but the port would require surgery.

I took my first treatment through a vein in my hand, but during my second treatment, after getting stuck several times to no avail, and not wanting to cancel my session, I opted for the PICC line. I found it to be much more comfortable. A PICC line is a thin, flexible tube that can be left in place for weeks or months once it's inserted, so you're not being stuck with needles every time you go for treatment. And with all the trouble I've had over the years with nurses finding a vein in my hands, I figured the fewer needle sticks, the better.

I sat in a padded, ivory "dentist" chair while the nurse hung a bag of liquid from a wheeled stand and connected a plastic tube to the needle in my vein. After receiving an anti-nausea drug for thirty minutes, I was given the Adriamycin, followed by the Cytoxan. While the medicine flowed into my body, Brett and I talked and watched the television on the wall. Out in the hall, I could hear other patients coming and going, and I wondered what kind of cancer had brought each of them to this place. From start to finish, I was at the clinic for only a couple of hours, but I know some treatments can take as long as eight hours to receive.

Brett and I left the clinic around seven o'clock. We came home to find a delicious meal waiting, prepared by friends from my Bible study. I was starving, so I heaped a plate with a lime gelatin salad and chicken enchiladas. An hour or so later, Brett and I were sitting on the sofa. He leaned toward me, his eyes soft with concern. "How do you feel?"

I gave him a big smile. "I feel great, don't worry. This is going to be a breeze."

I did feel great at nine. By eleven o'clock, though, I was sick as a dog—and to this day I get queasy at the thought of chicken enchiladas or lime gelatin.

I thought I would breeze through chemotherapy because I was strong, athletic, and healthy—aside from the cancer. But the chemo had other plans. The Compazine they'd given me didn't seem to help, and the steroids made me feel anxious. That first night, I tossed and turned in bed, throwing off the covers at one point, then pulling them up to my chin the next. I didn't have a fever, but I felt so nauseated that I couldn't sleep. I felt like every system in my body had mutinied and awakened me from a shallow doze just to tell me about it.

The next morning, I was so weak I could barely lift my head, but I had to get Breleigh ready for school. Somehow, by fitfully stopping and starting, I managed to get myself dressed. I pulled my hair back into a ponytail and stared at my pale face in the mirror. I had neither the desire nor the energy to apply makeup.

After resting on the bed for another five minutes, I stumbled to Breleigh's room, got her up, and after making sure she'd gotten dressed, fell back into bed while Brett drove her to school. I had absolutely no desire to eat—and I'm a girl who *likes* to eat. I spent half the day stretched out on the sofa, not quite believing that the chemo had knocked me so decisively off my feet.

The day after every chemo treatment, I had to go to the clinic to get a Neulasta shot. This drug is important because it helps the body produce white blood cells, which fight infection. If your white blood cell count goes below a certain level, you can't get your next treatment—and it's important to get your treatments on time. I don't know how I did it, but I managed to get to the clinic that morning to get my injection. I wanted to stay on schedule and get this cancer treatment behind me.

On Wednesday, I didn't want to do anything, but we had planned to go to a friend's house to celebrate Thanksgiving, and I had promised to make cornbread dressing, a Southern specialty. If I was going to get the dressing made, I had to do it that afternoon.

Once when we were eating at a steak house, I heard a woman ask the waiter how anyone could eat a thirty-two-ounce steak. "Easy," the young man answered. "You eat it bite by bite."

That's how I made my cornbread dressing. I got up, pulled out the recipe, and as a wave of nausea rose, I went to lie down on the sofa. After a few minutes, I went back into the kitchen, set out the ingredients, and staggered back to the sofa. When I had gathered my strength again, I poured the cornmeal into the bowl, added the other ingredients (trying not to inhale the scent), and then went back to the living room.

What should have taken ten minutes to mix took all afternoon, but by dinnertime I had a dish of cornbread dressing in the oven.

On Thanksgiving, we went to the home of the friends we've always considered our Green Bay family. I set the dressing on the table with the other dishes, then apologized and said I was going to lie down on their sofa. I felt miserable, but I couldn't imagine spending Thanksgiving alone in my bedroom. During the meal, I sat at the table and picked at my food for about ten minutes, then went back to the living room. Fortunately, these friends were close enough to understand what I was going through.

I struggled all that week. I didn't care if I ate or drank, but I knew I needed to drink plenty of liquids because the Adriamycin is hard on your kidneys. Problem was, I couldn't drink water; all I wanted was Coke. I also knew I needed to eat in order to keep up my strength, but

My first round of chemo had taught me just how strong I wasn't.

the only appetite I had came from the steroids, and the only food I wanted was Campbell's chicken noodle soup.

What does chemotherapy actually *feel* like? Like a bad flu, but without the fever. The nausea is the worst thing, but there's also a general achy feeling (from the Neulasta shot), tender skin, pain in the joints, and a deep, overwhelming fatigue.

I felt awful from Monday through Friday, but by Saturday I started to feel like my old self. I decided to run a few errands—to the grocery store and to the Packers Pro Shop to pick up a jersey and a few balls for Brett to autograph for an upcoming charity auction. By the time I got home, I was exhausted again. When my mother called to see how I was doing, I had to admit the truth. Though two weeks earlier I'd told her to stay in Mississippi because I was going to "tough it out" on chemo, this time I meekly told her she could come to Green Bay if she wanted to. My first round of chemo had taught me just how strong I *wasn't*.

By the next week, I had regained enough strength to resume my exercise routine for three days. By the end of the week, my strength had fully returned—and just in time. When the next Monday rolled around, I went back to the clinic for my second round of treatments.

Learning the ropes in round two

Brittany, who'd come up to Green Bay for a Packer game on the weekend, went with me to my second chemo treatment. When I first went in, the nurse had a hard time finding a vein. After about six sticks, she was going to send me home and tell me to come back the next day, but I wanted to press on. I asked for a PICC line instead, and learned that the insertion is a relatively simple procedure.

The PICC tubing is inserted into one of the large veins of the arm near the bend of the elbow. After the insertion area is numbed with a special anesthetic cream, a needle is inserted and the PICC is threaded through it into the vein until the tip rests just above the heart. The other end of the PICC remains outside the body and is capped when not in use.[3]

With a PICC line in place, a patient can be given chemo,

antibiotics, and intravenous fluids without risk of blowing a surface vein that may have hardened due to previous chemo treatment. A nurse can even take a blood sample through a PICC line.

I went up to the ultrasound unit, where the radiologist inserted the narrow tube into my upper arm. It only took

FIGHTING FATIGUE

If you are undergoing chemo or radiation, you will probably feel some kind of fatigue—it's the most common side effect reported by cancer patients. The following are some ways you can cope with a lack of energy.

- Prioritize your day. Make a list of the most important things you have to do, and rejoice if you get one item crossed off your list. Don't sweat the small stuff.

- Include rest breaks in your daily schedule. Remember how I made that cornbread dressing by resting between steps of the recipe? Don't assume you have to do everything in one effort.

- Learn how to enjoy catnaps. An extended nap can leave you feeling wiped out, but a twenty-minute doze might be just what the doctor ordered.

- Don't give up your favorite activities, but scale them down. Instead of spending the day at the mall, spend fifteen minutes browsing your favorite store.

- Take time for prayer and meditation every day. Spiritual refreshment is every bit as important as physical nourishment.

- Eat like a horse, not a hog. "Graze" in the kitchen by eating several mini-meals instead of three large ones.

about two minutes to insert, and it would make receiving my chemo treatments much easier.

To prevent the line from becoming blocked, a small amount of saline must be flushed into the line every day. A home health nurse came to the house to show me how to do it, but after that I was able to take care of the line myself. I learned to eat

- When you're in treatment, be content to get food into your system. When you're feeling better, try to eat a balanced diet and stay away from fatty foods.

- Be aware that you can lose muscle mass if you don't remain active. Try to weight train a couple of times a week during treatment, and the next week, when you're feeling stronger, you should definitely get in some lifting to maintain your muscle mass. Try to walk for half an hour three or four times a week, and then lift some free weights. Muscle cannot turn to fat—that's impossible—but you can lose muscle tone when you go through a period of inactivity.

- Don't be shy about asking others to help around the house or the office. Introduce your teens to the vacuum cleaner and help your husband write a grocery list.

- Drink plenty of fluids, especially water.

- Limit your caffeine and alcohol intake.

- Watch a comedy show you enjoy. Laughter really is good medicine. "A cheerful heart is good medicine, but a broken spirit saps a person's strength" (Proverbs 17:22).

- Keep a journal to record your deepest thoughts and prayers. The act of writing things down tends to clear our minds, and an untroubled mind rests easier.

lemons and salt while I was doing the flushing to lessen the taste of saline and the water-up-my-nose sensation.

Every method of insertion—through a vein, a PICC line, or a port—has advantages and disadvantages, but the PICC line worked beautifully for me. I kept it in for a couple of days after my last chemo treatment so they could take blood from it, and then we took it out. I felt no pain at all during the removal.

A woman's glory

During the two weeks that followed my first chemo treatment, I kept searching for signs of hair loss. No one at the clinic would tell me exactly when I might expect my hair to fall out, so every time I brushed my hair, I checked the bristles for clumps. So far, I hadn't noticed anything unusual.

When I went to the clinic for my second treatment, I asked again: "When might I expect my hair to fall out?" The doctor finally said that, for most people, hair loss usually begins the fourteenth day after the commencement of chemo, though everyone's experience was different.

I received the second treatment and went home, a little more at ease because I knew what to expect. I planned to spend the next week at home in my pajamas, writing thank-you letters for all the cards and gifts of encouragement I'd received. Most of them had come from breast cancer patients, and I tried to respond to all of them. I knew better than to plan anything strenuous for the next five days.

No one had told me that hair loss would hurt.

Sure enough, like clockwork, my scalp began to feel really sore that night. No one had told me that hair loss would *hurt*.

As a child, did you ever wear your hair in a tight pony-tail? When you released the ponytail and your hair settled back into its usual position, remember how your hair and scalp seemed to ache? Multiply that sensation by ten, and that's what my head felt like—one gigantic ponytail adjustment. Maybe it was my hair follicles resisting the inevitable, I don't know. But the next morning when I woke up, my cotton pillowcase looked like it had been transformed into black satin—it was *covered* in hair. I ran my fingertips through my hair and came away with a handful.

I drew a deep breath and steeled myself for the inevitable. I don't understand the allure of hair, but there's no denying that most women care deeply about it. Little girls drape bath towels over their heads and pretend to have long hair. They love the story of Rapunzel. And manufacturers have discovered that dolls don't sell well unless a child can indulge in what's known as "hair play." In 1992, the makers of Barbie produced a "totally hair" version, whose hair reached down to her toes. It became the best-selling Barbie ever.[4]

In 1548, Agnolo Firenzuola, author of *Delle bellezze delle Donna (On the Beauty of Women),* wrote, "However well-favored a lady may be, if she has not fine hair, her beauty is despoiled of all charm and glory."[5] Nancy Etcoff, in her book *Survival of the Prettiest,* tells us that more than half the women who answered a 1993 *Glamour* magazine survey agreed with these statements: "If my hair looks good, I feel attractive no matter what I'm wearing or how I look otherwise," and, "If my hair isn't right, nothing else can make me feel that I look good."[6]

Our hair tells the world a lot about us—not only the obvious things like our gender, age, taste, and attitude, but subtle things, too. Nancy Etcoff says, "If your hair falls past your shoulders it has been on your head for a couple of years. . . . It's giving signs of what we have eaten, what drugs we have taken, and provides a record of how our health has been for as long as it grows on our head. It's a bit disconcerting, but part of the beauty of long hair may be that it has a history, our history, written on it."[7]

When I was in high school, my hair was very thick, coarse, and wavy. At the time, I had no idea how to fix it or straighten it, but eventually I learned how to tame it. Since then, I've grown quietly proud of my long, thick hair. As I sat that morning in a growing cloud of it, I realized I had to do something. If I let it fall out naturally, I'd eventually have white patches of scalp showing through. At that moment, I didn't look bad, but soon I'd look worse than a hound with mange.

I called my hairdresser and asked if she'd be willing to shave my head. We met at a friend's house, and with a razor she gave me a buzz. I had thought about donating my hair to Locks of Love, but they need at least ten inches, and my hair hadn't completely grown out since the last time I had cut my hair for the donation program.

When I stepped outside, I realized I was going to go through a frigid Green Bay winter . . . bald.

When the clippers stopped humming, I drew a deep breath and looked in the mirror. I don't think there's any way to prepare for the shock of seeing your bare scalp for the first time—my head seemed so *white* against my tanned face and dark brows.

"It looks good," my friend said, trying to be supportive. "You have the best-shaped head. You look like Demi Moore in *G.I. Jane.*"

Really? Then why don't you shave your *head?*

I stifled my snide thought, thanked her for the compliment, and pulled on a little knit cap I'd brought with me. I didn't linger at the mirror.

When I stepped outside, I realized I was going to go

through a frigid Green Bay winter . . . bald. I would need to stock up on knit caps, and maybe even buy a wig or two. Fortunately, the Packers sell knit caps, and I knew where I could get a few.

When I got home, I went into the bathroom and pulled off my cap. In private, I held up a hand mirror, turned in

TO WIG *or not to wig?*

How do you cope with losing your hair during your cancer treatment? First of all, know that there is no "right" or "wrong" when it comes to how you proceed. Some women are confident enough to stride boldly and baldly into the public eye. Others are more comfortable with their heads covered by a wig, scarf, turban, or hat.

You may want to adopt a combination of methods—wearing a wig in public, for instance, and a stocking cap at home. Your choice will depend upon the weather where you live, your lifestyle, and your personality.

The following are tips from the National Cancer Institute:

- If you choose to cover your head, get your wig before you lose a lot of hair. You may be able to buy a wig at a specialty shop for cancer patients. Someone may even come to your home to help you with fitting and styling.

- You might want to consider borrowing a wig for an extended time. Check with the nurse to see about resources for free wigs in your community.

- Take your wig to your hairdresser or the shop where it was purchased for styling and cutting to frame your face.

- Some health insurance policies cover the cost of a hairpiece needed because of cancer treatment. A wig is also a tax-deductible expense. Be sure to check your policy and ask your doctor for a "wig prescription" for your tax records.[8] 🌿

113

front of the sink, and carefully checked the back and sides of my head.

My heart sank. No doubt about it: except for dozens of dark little pricklies that covered my scalp like peach fuzz, I was as bald as a kneecap.

I forced a smile and refused to cry. Chemotherapy and its side effects were part of my treatment. Being bald for a few months was a small price to pay for getting well.

The cancer had caught me by surprise, but I wasn't surprised by the hair loss. I knew it was coming, I was prepared, and I knew my hair would eventually grow back. Besides, hair is not what makes you who you are. It's not where true beauty comes from.

I decided that I wouldn't worry about it, but neither would I go out in public with a bald head. I wasn't ashamed of my bare scalp, but I didn't want people looking at me and thinking of me as sick. I didn't want pity.

Facing the world

When I went out to football games that season (I only missed two), I wore short little wigs covered by a Packer stocking cap. When members of the media asked me about losing my hair, I'd quip, "I have a few wigs, so if you see my husband out and about with a redhead, don't start any rumors. It'll be me."

At home, to ease the girls' fears, I wore fun wigs—blond or red. Those were inexpensive wigs that didn't look very good; I wore them just to have fun with my family. When I went out, I usually wore a wig with a cap pulled over it.

Once the season ended and we went home to Mississippi, though, it was too hot to wear a cap plus a wig. So I bought a good wig of real human hair and wore it to a couple of events—in fact, I wore it when I appeared on *Good Morning America* to promote an A&E program I'd done the summer before about sports wives.

I was on the show with three other ladies, so I wasn't nearly as nervous as I'd been when I was interviewed by Brad Goode from *Extra.* Charles Gibson, who had also had a bout with cancer, conducted the interview. I also got to visit with his co-host, Robin Roberts, a warm, friendly Southern

LOCKS OF LOVE, *a worthy charity*

Locks of Love is a public, nonprofit organization that provides hairpieces to financially disadvantaged children suffering from long-term medical hair loss. Brittany, Breleigh, and I have donated hair to this special program. If you would like to join us, you can visit their Web site at www.locksoflove.org for more information or simply keep the following in mind:

- Hair must be at least ten inches long, measured tip to tip. (Curly hair may be stretched.) Hair that is six to ten inches in length will be sold for fair market value and the income used to reduce costs.

- Hair must be in a ponytail or braid before it is cut. Colored or permed hair is usable; bleached hair is not.

- Hair must be clean and completely dry before it is mailed in. Place the ponytail or braid inside a plastic bag, then place the bag inside a padded envelope.

- Write your name and address on a separate sheet of paper and include inside the envelope.

- Mail hair donations to Locks of Love, 2925 10th Avenue N, Suite 102, Lake Worth, FL 33461.

girl from Pass Christian, Mississippi, which is only about twenty miles from Kiln. The interview itself was easy; the only worrisome aspect for me was the wig—I kept wondering whether everyone could tell I was wearing one. But if wearing a wig on TV could do something to provide hope and comfort to other women going through the same ordeal, then that was fine.

FOR HUSBANDS

Men, hearing a diagnosis that your wife has breast cancer can send *your* senses reeling, too.

I believe the most important thing you can do for your wife during breast cancer treatment is let her know that you're there for support. It's definitely important to stay positive and to encourage her to get through the day. Let her know it's okay for her to be sick and in bed for a couple of days. Do what you can to make things easier around the house. Look for little ways to encourage your wife, the way Brett and my girls encouraged me.

One thing Brett did was keep a running countdown of how many days remained in my cycles of chemotherapy treatment. "Hang in there," he'd tell me, "only fourteen days left!" The fact that he cared enough to count—and the knowledge that an end was in sight—meant so much to me. When I had a "down day," he'd remind me that I'd already come through X number of days, and I was almost at the finish line.

You can bet there was a lot of high-fiving at our house when that last day finally arrived!

Here are some tips to help you cope with your wife's diagnosis of breast cancer.

- Realize that even though you can't "fix things," *you are not helpless.* You have strength your spouse needs, and sometimes all she needs you to do is hold her hand.

Still, seeing my bald head was an odd experience for everyone at first. One morning, I was in the shower when Breleigh came into the bathroom. We have a glass door, so I knew she was looking at my head and thinking . . . *What?* I'd been wearing either a wig or a cap around the house, so she hadn't yet seen me bald.

I turned off the water, grabbed my towel, and asked

- Your spouse needs to know it's okay for her to be sick, unadorned, and not at her best. Let her know your commitment to her is not based on her looks.

- Tell her she's strong and you will be with her for the duration. Don't assume she knows this—verbalize your commitment.

- At the time of diagnosis, be strong and tell her she can beat the cancer. Later you will have time to share your fears. When cancer first strikes, your spouse needs your strength.

- It's okay to cry.

- The Family and Medical Leave Act guarantees you the right to accompany your spouse to doctors' appointments. (An eligible employee is granted up to twelve workweeks of unpaid leave in a twelve-month period.) If at all possible, go with her.

- *Be quiet and listen.* Many doctors and therapists believe this should be the breast cancer spouse's motto.[9]

- Tell her she is beautiful and you love her.

Breleigh to hand me a tube of lotion that was over on the tub. As she walked across the bathroom, her eyes remained locked on my head, and she had the most peculiar look on her face. When she brought me the lotion, she stood for a moment as if searching for words. Finally, she said, "Mommy, your hair looks really pretty."

I burst out laughing because there wasn't any hair. "Thanks, sweetie," I said, "but I know it really doesn't."

"I know," she said, grinning. "I was just kidding."

I realized that my five-year-old loved me enough to tell a white lie in order to make me feel better.

Right after I shaved my head, my girls cut their long hair for Locks of Love. I was touched that they'd make that gesture of support for me. I don't think my being bald bothered Brittany, but Breleigh had a bit of a hard time with it. I think she was worried about what other people would think. She usually wanted me to wear my wig when we went out. I think she was afraid that people would stare at me, and she didn't want me to be hurt.

Brittany, who occasionally came up to Green Bay for Brett's games and was often with us during my chemo treatments, made comments such as, "I think you look cool with no hair." I'm not sure I believed her, but I sure appreciated her encouragement.

I appreciated all the little things my children did to ease my awkwardness, but one of the sweetest gestures of support came from my husband. As soon as Brett knew I was about to lose my hair, he had someone at the stadium shave his head, and he surprised me with it at home that night.

I was touched, because I realized he was going to do whatever it took to help me get through this.

Brett was strong for me, providing a shoulder to cry on and all the support I needed, but it wasn't easy for him to be strong on *and* off the field. When he asked me if he should quit playing in order to devote more time to me, I said, "No, not because I have cancer. Never walk away from football because of me. I'll back whatever decision you make, but you can't quit because of me."

My entire family drew close to support me, and their presence and encouragement gave me a great sense of strength.

No perks?

Not only did I lose the hair on my scalp, but my dark brows thinned noticeably and I lost my eyelashes. I've always had long, thick lashes, so when they began to fall out, I didn't look anything like myself. To compensate, I penciled in my brows and applied my eyeliner a little thicker than usual. When it came to my lashes, I dutifully applied mascara. Even when I had only two lashes left, I gingerly brushed them with the mascara wand, determined to make the most of what I had without pulling those faithful lashes out!

With hair falling out all around me, I was hoping I'd lose the hair on my legs as well; but for some perverse reason, that hair wasn't affected by the chemo. Not having to shave my legs for several months would have been a nice perk.

No one warned me about this, but I found out that you can also lose your nails, a condition called onychomadesis.[10] The nail separates from the nail bed and falls off. A new nail will grow once the chemo is finished.

I lost a toenail on one foot and developed white (and, in some cases, black) lines in my fingernails. It all depends on how long and how aggressive your chemo treatment is, but chemo can be hard on your skin and your nails.

To give my nails a fighting chance, I wore nail polish to keep them strong, used gloves when doing household chores, and kept my nails clipped short for the duration of my treatment.[11]

Chemo brain

Sometimes I forget things and repeat myself. I do it more often now than before I went through chemo.

As I went through treatment, and even in the following months, I became aware of a condition that is common knowledge among patients: "chemo brain." Many observers—and even some experts—laugh when you mention chemo brain, probably assuming that cancer patients are blaming chemotherapy for the ordinary forgetfulness that seems to bedevil all adults as they grow older.

Chemo brain is a lot like menopause—people who have never experienced it tend to think it's all in the sufferer's head. But I know it's not, because I've experienced chemo brain, even though I didn't realize what it was until nearly a year after my treatments. Then I asked my doctor, and he said, "Oh, that's called 'chemo brain.'"

After receiving chemo, some patients tend to experience "word loss"—you'll find yourself searching for the simplest, most common word and you simply can't think of it. It's almost like you have adult-onset Attention Deficit Disorder. I'll find myself zoning out when I'm talking to someone, and conversations aren't as easy as they used to be. Even now, two years after my treatment, I find myself searching for ordinary words that elude me.

I was delighted to see an article on chemo brain in a recent edition of the *New York Times*. The article reported that one woman who'd had chemo filled the family water glasses with turkey gravy at a family dinner. Another could not remember how to subtract when balancing her checkbook.[12]

"Until recently," Dr. Daniel Silverman told the *Times* reporter, "oncologists would discount it, trivialize it, make patients feel it was all in their heads. Now there's enough literature, even if it's controversial, that not mentioning it as a possibility is either ignorant or an evasion of professional duty."[13]

Nearly all cancer survivors who've had chemotherapy will experience at least some short-term memory loss or cognitive loss. Fortunately, most people improve over time, but experts say that about 15 percent can be groping for words years later.[14] I'm nearly three years past my chemo treatments, and I feel as if my chemo brain condition is getting worse.

Research is continuing into the cause and cure for chemo brain, but perhaps we are fortunate to be facing the problem. "The new interest in chemo brain," says the *New York Times,* "is a testimony to enormous strides in the field. Patients who once would have died now live long enough to have cognitive side effects."[15]

Sometimes I forget things and repeat myself. But I'd rather stop and search for a word occasionally than not be around to watch my daughters grow up. I hope researchers find a way to make the problem less pervasive, but chemo brain is a small price to pay for surviving cancer.

Once, Christie and I were talking on the phone while she was at the drive-through window at Subway. She placed her order and paid for her food. Twenty minutes later, when she pulled up in her driveway, she said, "Oh, my goodness, D—I forgot to get my sandwich."

If I were to do something like that today, I could blame it on chemo brain. Christie can only blame it on the fact that she has been around me *way* too long!

the huddle

After my last chemo treatment in January 2005, I took a few days to rest, and then in February I went through twice-daily radiation treatments for twelve days. By this time, the football season was over and we were back in Hattiesburg. The treatment was supposed to last six weeks, but I didn't want to keep going to the hospital for another six weeks. If my body could take it, I told my radiation oncologist, I wanted two treatments a day so I could put all the treatments behind me.

I elected to have radiation only on the tumor site, not the entire breast. After talking to my doctors, I felt that procedure would be safe for me, though it's not advisable for everyone. Everything depends on the size and aggressiveness of the cancer.

Radiation treatments are generally pain free and of short duration—in fact, I found that we spent more time getting set up than I did receiving the actual radiation. Each treatment lasted only a few minutes, and the entire session lasted less than half an hour. After the setup, I sat under the X-ray machine while a technician monitored me on a closed-circuit television. I was always able to communicate with her, however, so I never felt alone.

Some side effects associated with radiation are hair loss in the treated area, fatigue, nausea, loss of appetite, and a rash or redness in the treatment area. Most of these side effects are temporary and pass quickly. I had no side effects like burning of the skin, but the treatments were exhausting. I remember sitting on the sofa a couple of nights in my little stocking cap, looking over at Brett, and bursting into tears. That's unusual for me, because I don't usually break down in a crisis.

I remember sitting on the sofa a couple of nights in my little stocking cap, looking over at Brett, and bursting into tears.

These were the strangest episodes, because I'm not a crier by nature. I would sit on the couch with tears flowing down my face and not even be able to explain why I was crying. I would simply feel depressed and down, and my body would be drained of all energy.

I think it is especially hard for a woman when she's depressed and fatigued, because we're the caregivers, and normally the ones in charge of the home. I felt as if I had entered a slump I would never pull out of, and I had to surrender my caregiver role and let someone take care of me. It was hard to give up, and I didn't want to, but I simply ran out of fuel and lost my desire to get through the moment.

At times like that, I had to learn how to surrender, relax, and rest. It's part of the battle. Eventually, I regained my strength and pulled myself out of that slump, but there's no denying that exhaustion and illness are an emotional, mental, and physical battle.

In those times, Brett's strength and the prayers of hundreds of people pulled me through. Brett went public with my breast cancer battle right after we realized it was on the AP wire, so I received hundreds of cards and letters from people who assured me of their support.

When I was first diagnosed, however, I shut down and pulled away from everyone. I didn't want people to see me sick. It was almost as if I'd be exposing my weakness, and I didn't want them to see me that way. I didn't want anyone to see my depression and all my ragged emotions out on public display.

I stopped going to my Bible study during treatment, but those people continued to check on me and pray for me. I could feel their prayers. I also received thousands of letters from Packer fans around the country who were praying for me. I was always so grateful for those prayers, because they supported me when I had no strength left.

My Bible study group in Hattiesburg did something special to remind me of the power of prayer. Each woman picked a Bible verse to encourage me. An artist then took their handwritten verses and arranged them around a copy of Philippians 4:13: "For I can do everything through Christ, who gives me strength." I have placed the final framed art in my office, where every day it reminds me of this precious promise and my dear friends.

Recently, my co-author, Angela Hunt, heard a story about Francis Joseph Cardinal Spellman, archbishop of New York from 1939 to 1967. During a conversation with a businessman in a busy New York post office, Cardinal Spellman happened to mention that he was feeling tired.

"Tell me, Your Eminence," asked the businessman, "with all the work you do, do you ever get so tired that you forget to say your prayers at night?"

Spellman smiled. "When I'm so tired I can't keep my eyes

TWELVE
breast cancer myths exposed[1]

Myth: Only women with a family history of cancer get breast cancer.
Truth: Having a family history increases your risk, but 90 percent of women who get breast cancer have no family history of breast cancer.

Myth: Finding a lump in your breast means you definitely have breast cancer.
Truth: Eight out of ten lumps are benign—not cancerous. Do not let the appearance of a lump frighten you to the point that you're afraid to see a doctor.

Myth: Men do not get breast cancer.
Truth: This year, 1,600 men will be diagnosed with breast cancer. The cancer is rare in men, but it does occur.

Myth: Only women in their forties and fifties get breast cancer.
Truth: I was thirty-five when my breast cancer was diagnosed, and doctors recommend that all women have a mammogram at age thirty-five. I'm amazed that some doctors still advise patients to have a baseline mammogram at forty—I think you should have it early. I had no family history of cancer yet was diagnosed at age thirty-five. I'm no medical expert, but I highly recommend getting a baseline mammogram at age thirty-five and making sure you do regular breast self-exams at home.

I took chemo with several women even younger than I was. You are never too young to examine your breasts for changes!

Myth: Antiperspirants and deodorants can cause breast cancer.
Truth: An urban legend traveling over the Internet claims that the leading cause of breast cancer is clogged pores in the underarm area. This is simply not true. If it were, why do more breast cancers occur in the left breast?

Myth: Mammograms can cause breast cancer to spread.

Truth: A mammogram is simply an X-ray of the breast. Mammography is the best way to spot a cancerous growth, and it could save your life.

Myth: If you are cancer-free five years after being treated, you are cured from breast cancer.

Truth: Though some cancers can be considered "cured" after five years, breast cancer can recur at any time.

Myth: A high-fat diet can cause breast cancer.

Truth: A high-fat diet is not good for you, but it has not been directly linked to breast cancer.

Myth: If you're at high risk for breast cancer, there's nothing you can do about it.

Truth: There are several ways to reduce your risk of breast cancer, though you cannot eliminate all risk. One way to reduce your risk is by changing your lifestyle (e.g., minimize alcohol consumption, stop smoking, and incorporate regular exercise into your week).

Myth: An injury to the breast can cause breast cancer.

Truth: An injury to the breast may result in the *detection* of breast cancer, but it will not cause it.

Myth: Only large-breasted women get breast cancer.

Truth: Every woman has some risk of breast cancer, regardless of her race, breast size, or socioeconomic status. Even women who have had their breasts removed still have some risk because some breast tissue remains.

Myth: If you get breast cancer, you will probably die.

Truth: A diagnosis of breast cancer is not a death sentence. Though breast cancer is the second leading cause of cancer death in women (after lung cancer), the majority of women who were diagnosed with breast cancer five years ago are still alive. ❧

open, I simply say, 'Dear God, you know I've been working in your vineyard all day. If you don't mind, could we skip the details till morning?'"[2]

I know exactly how Cardinal Spellman felt. When I was too exhausted to pray, I simply thanked God for all the people who were praying for me. Whenever I had a bad day, I would remember those prayers and feel my strength begin to return. Most days, however, I felt as if I were in the center of an incredible calm.

I lived out the truths found in Philippians 4:6-7: "Don't worry about anything; instead, pray about everything. Tell God what you need, and thank him for all he has done. Then you will experience God's peace, which exceeds anything we can understand. His peace will guard your hearts and minds as you live in Christ Jesus."

Praying for the sick

Prayer has always been a big part of my life. Knowing that the people in my Bible study, my family and friends in Wisconsin and Mississippi, and people I'd never even met were praying for me every day meant the world to me. I'm no theologian, but I have learned a few things about prayer and healing.

When someone is desperately sick with a serious disease like cancer, it's natural for anyone who has even a smattering of religious belief to immediately turn to prayer. Nothing can make us feel quite as helpless as cancer, and human nature compels us to reach out for help. When we don't know exactly what causes a disease, and when we can never be 100 percent certain we have defeated it, God is the only one who can give us genuine peace and comfort.

But *how* do we pray? In the Bible, the apostle James gives us instructions. He says, "Are any of you sick? You should call for the elders of the church to come and pray over you, anointing you with oil in the name of the Lord. Such a prayer offered in faith will heal the sick, and the Lord will make you well. And if you have committed any sins, you will be forgiven."[3]

But are we supposed to take his words literally? Are we supposed to call for a minister, splash the sick person with Wesson oil, and start praying? And why does James bring up the matter of sins?

Perhaps those verses make you uncomfortable because they remind you of faith healers on TV who smack desperate people on the forehead and lay them out on the floor. Or perhaps you've known someone who died from a disease, and later you heard people saying the person wasn't healed because he or she didn't have enough faith.

How can we know that our prayers will make any difference with God?

Again, I'm not an expert, but Angela, who is about to complete her doctorate in theology, points out that James indicates it is the *elders'* faith, not the sick person's, that makes a difference in healing.

These elders, or mature Christians, are to offer prayers "of faith." What does that mean? Faith is more than wishful thinking or even sincere conviction. Faith is a confident trust in God, which is based on a relationship with him.

Our girls could ask Brett for anything, and if it's within his power and beneficial for them, he would move mountains to answer their request. Why? Because he's their daddy and he loves them.

If you are a child of God, the same relationship exists between you and the Almighty. He wants to answer your prayers because he loves you.

But what's this business about sin?

Let's suppose you work for your dad at a warehouse. You're

pulling the night shift, but you called in sick last Friday night and went to a movie instead of going to work. While you were standing in the popcorn line, you saw your dad coming out of another theater. He saw you, too, but he didn't confront you.

On Monday afternoon, you're back at your station, and you desperately need a raise. Do you go to your dad's office and start talking salary right away?

Of course not. You know that *he* knows that you lied about being sick Friday night. Before you can ask him for a favor, you're going to have to confess, apologize, and repair the injured relationship. You have to clear the air between you. Your dad loves you, and his desire to do good things for you is not at all diminished by your sin, but he wants you to grow up to be a steady, mature worker, and he can't reward bad behavior. Only if you show signs of progress is he likely to consider your request for a raise.

The situation James describes isn't much different. As we draw near to God to pray for healing—for ourselves or for someone else—we need to make sure that our relationship with him has not been marred by our disobedience or disinterest. And that's when we understand how loving God is: When we draw close to him, he draws close to us (see James 4:8). Our sins are forgiven and our prayers are heard.

Unanswered prayers

But what about those sincere Christians who pray over and over for someone—and then the person doesn't survive? How can we believe in prayer when not everyone we pray for is healed?

That's a tough question, and thousands of people have asked it. Angela lost her mother-in-law, Jean, after five years of battling breast cancer. Scores of faith-filled Christians prayed for Jean, but she died.

Why didn't God answer those prayers?

He did . . . but sometimes his answer is not what we hope for or expect.

If every one of our prayers were answered in the way we chose, what would God be like? A mature, loving father or a wishy-washy dad who's so desperate for approval that he spoils his kids? We've all seen young parents who are dominated by a willful toddler. I've even seen households that are dominated by spoiled dogs!

Do you expect the all-knowing, all-powerful God to be at your beck and call? Do we want him to be a "celestial bellboy" who runs to do our bidding?

I don't think so. Any god who would let me dictate to him wouldn't be much of a god. I don't know what lies around the next corner, but God does. And the Bible tells us again and again that he arranges all things *according to his sovereign will.*[4]

The reason for "unanswered prayers" lies in those last five words. The apostle John writes, "And we are confident that he hears us whenever we ask for anything that pleases him. And since we know he hears us when we make our requests, we also know that he will give us what we ask for."[5]

For our prayers to be answered with a *yes,* we must "ask for anything that pleases him." Yet how can we know what will please God? To know him well, we must remain close to him; we have to be involved in an intimate relationship with him, and we have to obey his commands.

When Jesus gave us the model prayer sometimes called the Lord's Prayer, he included these words: "May your will be done on earth, as it is in heaven."[6]

In other words, we can ask for anything, but we must be

willing to assert that we want God's will to be accomplished more than we want the thing we're requesting.

In his book *Prayer: Does It Make Any Difference?* Philip Yancey points out that Paul, Job, and even Jesus offered what we could call "unanswered prayers." Paul, the great missionary, had a physical weakness that God did not remove, Job's suffering continued for an extended time, and Jesus went to the cross despite his dread of the physical pain.[7]

I've learned at least one important thing through my bout with cancer and tragedy: everything happens for a reason. Even when I can't see the reason, God can.

As a child in Northern Ireland, missionary Amy Carmichael learned that God answers prayer in unexpected ways. One night, filled with hope, she asked God to take her ordinary brown eyes and change them to a bright blue to match her mother's.

The next morning the little girl bounded out of bed and pushed a chair over to the dressing table. She peered into the mirror, fully expecting to see that she had been given bright blue eyes . . . but they were still as brown as ever. God had not answered her prayer, so she decided she would never pray again.

"Even as she made this bitter resolve," writes biographer Nancy Robbins, "she seemed to hear a quiet voice saying somewhere, 'God said "no." Isn't "no" an answer?' She had to admit that 'no' can be an answer, and decided that perhaps it would be silly to stop praying just because God said 'no' once."[8]

Years later, when Amy established a home in India for little girls who had been cast away from their families, she realized why God had given her brown eyes in the first place. When out in public, she would often wear Indian attire and stain her arms and hands with coffee so that she could visit places where foreign women were not allowed. Blue eyes would have immediately aroused suspicion. Brown eyes enabled her to fit in and help the people she'd come to serve.

I've learned at least one important thing through my bout with cancer and tragedy: everything happens for a reason. Even when I can't see the reason, God can.

The sovereignty of God

"Sovereignty" is just a theological way of saying that God is in control of *everything*. He keeps the universe spinning in the heavens, he preserves our planet, and he upholds our lives. In Colossians, we learn that the world was created through Jesus, and "he holds all creation together."[9]

Not only does Jesus hold creation together, but our heavenly Father feeds the birds of the air, and not a single sparrow can fall to the ground without God's knowing about it.[10] "The very hairs on your head are all numbered," Jesus said. "So don't be afraid; you are more valuable to God than a whole flock of sparrows."[11]

God even knows—and cares—when the number of hairs on my head drops from 110,000 to 150. He knows and cares when there's nothing on my head but peach fuzz.

People have written entire books on why bad things happen to good people, and I can't pretend that I have all the answers as to why my family has been hit with so many tragedies and tough situations. But I do know this: though some people may look at a tragic event and say that God is cruel to allow such a thing, I don't believe God is cruel. I know that my attitude in life is based on my perspective, and because I believe in the kindness of God, I can trust his heart. After all, when I ask my children to do a chore they don't want to do, they may think of me as cruel. But I'm going to ask anyway, because I know that working around the house is good for their character.

Angela recently drew my attention to the words of David, the psalmist and king of Israel, who understood exactly how God ordered the events of his life. Writing under the inspiration of the Holy Spirit, David says:

O Lord, you have examined my heart
    and know everything about me.
You know when I sit down or stand up.
    You know my thoughts even when I'm far away.
You see me when I travel
    and when I rest at home.
    You know everything I do.
You know what I am going to say
    even before I say it, Lord.
You go before me and follow me.
Such knowledge is too wonderful for me,
    too great for me to understand!

I can never escape from your Spirit!
    I can never get away from your presence!
If I go up to heaven, you are there;
    if I go down to the grave, you are there.
If I ride the wings of the morning,
    if I dwell by the farthest oceans,
even there your hand will guide me,
    and your strength will support me.
I could ask the darkness to hide me
    and the light around me to become night—
    but even in darkness I cannot hide from you.
To you the night shines as bright as day.
    Darkness and light are the same to you.

You made all the delicate, inner parts of my body
    and knit me together in my mother's womb.

Thank you for making me so wonderfully complex!
    Your workmanship is marvelous—how well I know it.
You watched me as I was being formed in utter seclusion,
    as I was woven together in the dark of the womb.
You saw me before I was born.
    Every day of my life was recorded in your book.
Every moment was laid out
    before a single day had passed.

How precious are your thoughts about me, O God.
    They cannot be numbered!
I can't even count them;
    they outnumber the grains of sand!
And when I wake up,
    you are still with me![12]

I love the assurances in that psalm. Every day of my life, even the darkest, has been recorded in God's book. Every moment was laid out before I took my first breath.

God knows—and he has always known—what I would face in this life. He allows the dark days because he knows that those are the situations in which my character is formed, enlarged, and refined.

The apostle James wrote the following encouragement to Christians scattered throughout the world:

"Dear brothers and sisters, when troubles come your way, consider it an opportunity for great joy. For you know that when your faith is tested, your endurance has a chance to grow. So let it grow, for when your endurance is fully developed, you will be perfect and complete, needing nothing."[13]

I do not believe that I got cancer because of bad luck. I don't believe anything "just happens." Over and over the

Bible tells me that God moves the hearts of men and controls the fate of kings. I do not always understand why he allows certain tragedies, but I know I can trust him.

Everything happens for a reason.

And God knows the reasons.

Pray persistently

So . . . if God's going to do what he's going to do, why bother to pray? Because the Bible tells us that prayer is often the means through which God works his will.

As Angela pointed out to me, the book of James says, "You want what you don't have, so you scheme and kill to get it. You are jealous of what others have, but you can't get it, so you fight and wage war to take it away from them. Yet you don't have what you want because you don't ask God for it. And even when you ask, you don't get it because your motives are all wrong—you want only what will give you pleasure."[14]

We are to ask God for what we want and need, but we must be willing to desire his will most of all.

Jesus told a story that illustrates another reason we should pray:

> *Suppose you went to a friend's house at midnight, wanting to borrow three loaves of bread. You say to him, "A friend of mine has just arrived for a visit, and I have nothing for him to eat." And suppose he calls out from his bedroom, "Don't bother me. The door is locked for the night, and my family and I are all in bed. I can't help you." But I tell you this—though he won't do it for friendship's sake, if you keep knocking long enough, he will get up and give you whatever you need because of your shameless persistence.*

*And so I tell you, keep on asking, and you will receive
what you ask for. Keep on seeking, and you will find.
Keep on knocking, and the door will be opened to you.
For everyone who asks, receives. Everyone who seeks,
finds. And to everyone who knocks, the door will be
opened.*

*You fathers—if your children ask for a fish, do you
give them a snake instead? Or if they ask for an egg, do
you give them a scorpion? Of course not! So if you sinful
people know how to give good gifts to your children, how
much more will your heavenly Father give the Holy Spirit
to those who ask him.*[15]

When we pray persistently, God asks us to trust him to know what we need and when we need it. Sometimes he answers, "No." Sometimes he answers, "Wait." Sometimes he answers, "Yes."

Sometimes as we pray, we are the ones who are changed. As we draw closer to God, our desires and priorities shift— and those changes in us may be the answer to someone else's prayers, or even our own.

So whether you pray silently or loudly, don't be afraid to express your deepest feelings to God.

He loves you and wants to be close to you.

He is not unfeeling, and he is willing to forgive.

He is not afraid of your feelings or surprised by your questions.

He is not too far away to hear.

And he will answer you.

more than a game

You might not know that the Green Bay Packers are unique among NFL teams for several reasons. First of all, Green Bay is the smallest NFL city—and the place really does have a small-town atmosphere.

Second, the colder it gets up here, the more the fans like it. It could be zero degrees, with a minus-twenty windchill factor, and they'd still show up at Lambeau Field two hours before kickoff. Brett says they treat frostbite as if it were a badge of honor, giving new meaning to the phrase "true blue."

Third, the fans actually own the team. The Packers are the only publicly owned, nonprofit team in professional sports. Most of the stockholders are fans, and they own shares not to make a profit, but because they love to support their team—and its players.

Four thousand fans will show up to watch a minicamp workout. They pack Lambeau even when the temperature is below zero. The people of Green Bay are good people, and they constantly prove it. When Reggie White's church, the Inner City Church in Knoxville, Tennessee, burned down, the people of Green Bay raised more than a quarter of a million dollars to help rebuild it.

As much as we appreciate the support we get from nearly everyone in Green Bay, when we're there we always feel a bit like we're living in a fishbowl. Brett and I can barely go out to eat without being interrupted for autograph requests or people who want him to pose for a picture. Now that camera phones are popular, the problem has become even worse!

Sometimes, if we're lucky, we can sneak into the back of a movie theater, but even then we're likely to be recognized while we're standing in line at the door. I'm grateful my husband is so loved, but it'd also be nice from time to time to go out anonymously like everyone else.

I know that a lot of people think we Favres have the perfect life, but there are always sacrifices to be made. Our girls have often found it hard to have a famous dad who can't go to a school event as an ordinary parent.

A reporter for *USA Today* said that Brett has lived "not in a fishbowl, but in an aquarium where the sharks lurk on the outside and faces press endlessly against the glass, always eager for feeding time."[1]

Right after my breast cancer was diagnosed, I wasn't happy to learn that news of my condition had already been reported on the AP newswire. I was most concerned about my mother, whom I didn't tell right away because my diagnosis came so soon after Casey's death. But once the news hit the wire, I had to call Mom and give her the details. At that point, I wondered, *Why does everyone have to care about what's going on with us?*

After thinking about it a while, I realized that public attention had the potential to be a positive thing. The district attorney in Green Bay was going through breast cancer at the same time and doing her job without wearing a wig. Public reaction was mixed, but I thought she was a great role model. On the other hand, could I go to a Packer game with a bare head and face television cameras for a national broadcast?

I wasn't so sure about that.

The unblinking eye

When tragedy strikes our family, we are expected to grieve in public. The world watched us weep for Irvin and Casey; reporters from all over the country took notes on the off-hand comments we made about my breast cancer. It's not that we don't appreciate the attention or the fans or the media who are doing their jobs—because we do. We're grateful for the NFL and the many good years we've had in this job. I'm thrilled that my husband is healthy enough to play a game he still enjoys. But like everything else in life, there are trade-offs.

The first year we went to the Super Bowl, we received death threats in the mail. People would write Brett and say, "You don't deserve to have Deanna and Brittany live." That same year, before the Dallas game, we received so many threats that Brett had to have security guards stationed around him. We started using our security system at the house, and bodyguards escorted us to the Super Bowl.

It's bizarre, but we've had people walk up to the house and ask for a tour. One woman came to our house in Green Bay and knocked on the door. Brittany was home alone, and because the woman had five children with her, Britt assumed she was harmless. When Britt opened the door, the woman asked for Brett. Brittany told her he was playing golf.

The woman drove to the golf course and sent someone

out to tell Brett that his wife was waiting in the parking lot. Because I would never go to the course unless some emergency had come up, Brett went flying up to the parking lot. When he saw the woman who was waiting, he told the boy who'd come to get him that she wasn't his wife. But she was still waiting when Brett and Bus finished playing golf. As they hurried to get their clubs in the truck, she called out to Brett and said that God had told her they were soul mates and he was married to the wrong person.

The woman was obviously unbalanced. When Brett warned the Packers' management about her, he discovered that they'd been getting calls about her as well. Apparently, she'd been going through the town telling everyone that she and Brett Favre would soon be together.

I was beginning to wonder if—and how—she was planning to get rid of me.

Brett and I aren't the only ones who feel the sting of unwanted attention. After the Packers lost to New Orleans one year, Brittany's teacher walked into her classroom on Monday and said, "Man, the team must be pretty bad if the Saints beat them."

Ouch. What people don't seem to realize is that comments like that mean something personal to us. A snide comment about Brett is an attack against Brittany's dad. For most Americans, football is only a game, a fun way to spend a Sunday afternoon or a Monday night. But Packer football is a central part of our lives. The players and coaches are our *family*.

For most Americans, football is only a game, a fun way to spend a Sunday afternoon or a Monday night. But Packer football is a central part of our lives. The players and coaches are our family.

Besides, a comment like that isn't fair. That's like going up to a surgeon's son and saying, "Boy, your dad must not be a very good doctor because he lost that patient last weekend."

How unfair is that?

Breleigh is young, but she's not too young to feel pressure, too. She's especially sensitive, and not long ago two kids in the school cafeteria pulled her aside and said, "Your dad stinks. He's not a good football player."

I didn't know this was going on nearly every week, but I noticed that she started watching the games with an unusual focus on the score. "Mom," she'd ask, her gaze darting toward the scoreboard, "are we going to win?"

She worried every week and got to the point where she'd start to cry if the other team pulled ahead. "Mom," she'd say, looking at me with fear in her eyes, "are we going to lose again?"

For nearly an entire season, I watched Breleigh wear herself to an emotional frazzle during every game. While I was at the game, she'd watch at home and call me on my cell phone after every touchdown. If we scored, she'd be thrilled, but if the other team scored, she'd be a nervous wreck.

I felt horrible. I had no idea why she was carrying on about the score until one day she asked, "Was Daddy a good football player a long time ago?"

That's when I realized someone else was telling her things and causing all her anxiety. I got the full story from her and went to the school to talk to the principal about the boys who were giving her a hard time in the cafeteria. The principal caught the boys and made them apologize. That helped Breleigh a lot, but the pressure of football weekends can still stress her out.

When Brett retires, I will enjoy reclaiming some of our privacy and having people not care so much about what we're doing or saying. It'll be nice to turn on the sports channel during football season and not hear a debate with someone defending my husband while another person is criticizing him. We try not to watch the sports channel right now, because whether or not anyone else will admit it, it's not fun to hear negative comments about someone you love. I'll be glad when that part of this life is over.

I know there will always be a group that will recognize Brett and want to come up to him. Maybe that's why we enjoy being at home, playing games, and having fun in a private setting. Every year, we take the family to Disney World—we've been doing it since Brittany was five—and I hope we can keep doing that, even after our girls have families of their own.

But we are truly happiest when we are home, surrounded by family, and wearing comfortable clothes. In the winter, I wear jogging suits to work out and run errands. I'm comfortable that way. Who wants to put on makeup and be decked out every day? Not me.

Brett favors jeans and T-shirts, and he's been known to tease his friends about dressing up. One time Gilbert Brown, a big Packers defensive lineman, was getting on a plane to go to a game. Brett was already in his seat, and when Gilbert boarded the plane in a green suit with a green top hat, Brett's first thought was *pool table*. As Gilbert walked by, Brett looked up and said, "Eight ball, corner pocket."

When all the guys erupted in laughter, Gilbert grinned and said, "Man, I'll never wear this suit again."

Another time, Brett was in a quarterbacks meeting and Doug Pederson came in with a button-up shirt that had fish on it. Brett took one look and quipped, "Did that shirt come with a singing bass?" Doug never wore the shirt again, and his wife, Jeannie, gave Brett an earful for making fun of Doug's wardrobe.

Me at 8 months

My mom has always been my spiritual role model. Here we are in front of our old church, Infant of Prague, on the day of my First Communion.
1976

My cousin Robin was like a sister to me growing up
4th grade

Me holding my little sister, Christie. We have always been very close!
1975

That's my little brother, Casey, in the locket around my neck
7th grade

Me at center court. Check out the high-tops!
7th grade

Brett and me at his senior prom
1987

*Brittany and me
on our way to cheer
for Brett at USM*
1989

↑ **ABOVE**
*Brett and me celebrating USM's
victory over Alabama*
1990

Brittany (age 2) and me
1991

high school & college

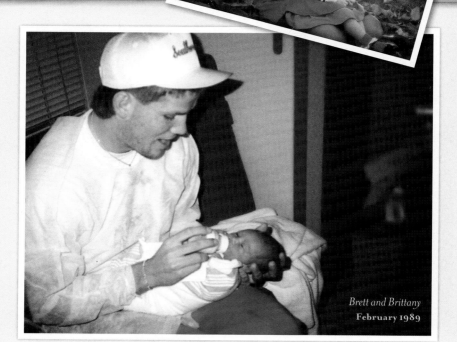

Brett and Brittany
February 1989

Our wedding day
July 14, 1996

Brittany and Brett
at St. Agnes Church.
She was sooo excited!

our wedding

"Oh sure, make me do all the work!"

RIGHT →
*Maybe not one of my best pictures, but definitely
one of my best days! Me with baby Breleigh.*
July 13, 1999

← **LEFT**
*Britt and Breleigh with Mama Bo
(Bonita) and Poppy (Irvin) Favre*

Brett and Breleigh

The "4" of us at Lambeau Field
1999

our growing family

The Favre family
with Jazzy the dog
2000

Christie, Mom, and me
1996

Christie, Casey, and me
1998

Brittany and me
December 2006

The Favre Clan, *from left: Jade (Jeff and Rhonda's daughter), Jeff (Brett's brother), Aunt KK (Irvin's sister), Rhonda (Jeff's wife), Dylan (Jeff and Rhonda's son), Breleigh, Brett, me, Brittany, Irvin, Bonita, MeMaw, Brandi (Brett's sister), Morgan (Scott's wife), and Scott (Brett's brother)*
Christmas 2001

*I know one of God's blessings is
that my brother will always live on
through his son, Casey*
2006

↓ **BELOW**
Breleigh with Uncle Casey
2003

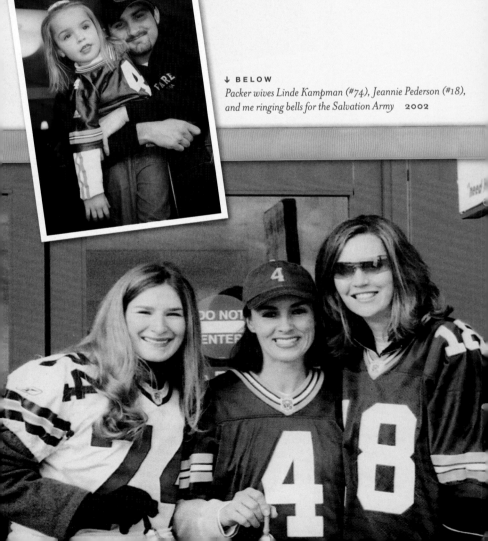

↓ **BELOW**
*Packer wives Linde Kampman (#74), Jeannie Pederson (#18),
and me ringing bells for the Salvation Army* 2002

Poppy and Breleigh.
What a pair!
2003

Mom, Brittany, me, Dad,
Christie, Josh (Christie's husband),
and Casey at Super Bowl XXXII
in San Diego
1998

Casey and me
2003

At home in Mississippi
2003

Breleigh and me at Lambeau Field
2004

Bre, Brett and Britt.
This is one of my favorite pictures
of my most valuable people!
2001

Breleigh and me at home in Mississippi
September 2004

Brett and me on the field after a win in New England
2002

RIGHT →
Brett and I are escorted off the field
after the Oakland Monday night game
December 22, 2003

Brett's dad would have been
so proud of him that night.
I know I was.

the best of times . . . and the worst

↑ **ABOVE**
Bonita and me at the ESPY Awards
July 2004

← LEFT
Accepting Brett's ESPY Award for "Best Moment"
2004

RIGHT →
The Favre girls
September 2004

The four of us at home in Mississippi
2004

RIGHT →
Brett and me at the annual
Favre Fourward Foundation
celebrity softball tournament
in Green Bay
June 2004

Me, my dad, and my sister, about three weeks into my chemotherapy treatment
December 2004

The girls and me at Lambeau Field a year after my diagnosis
2005

Me with Charles Gibson, after my appearance on Good Morning America
2005

We love you!
"Your Team"

"My team" at the Van Dyke Haebler Center at Columbia St. Mary's Hospital in Milwaukee
(from left: Thomas Berns, MD; Deb Theine, RN; me; radiologist Patrick McWey, MD;
and mammography technician Pam Piel)
2005

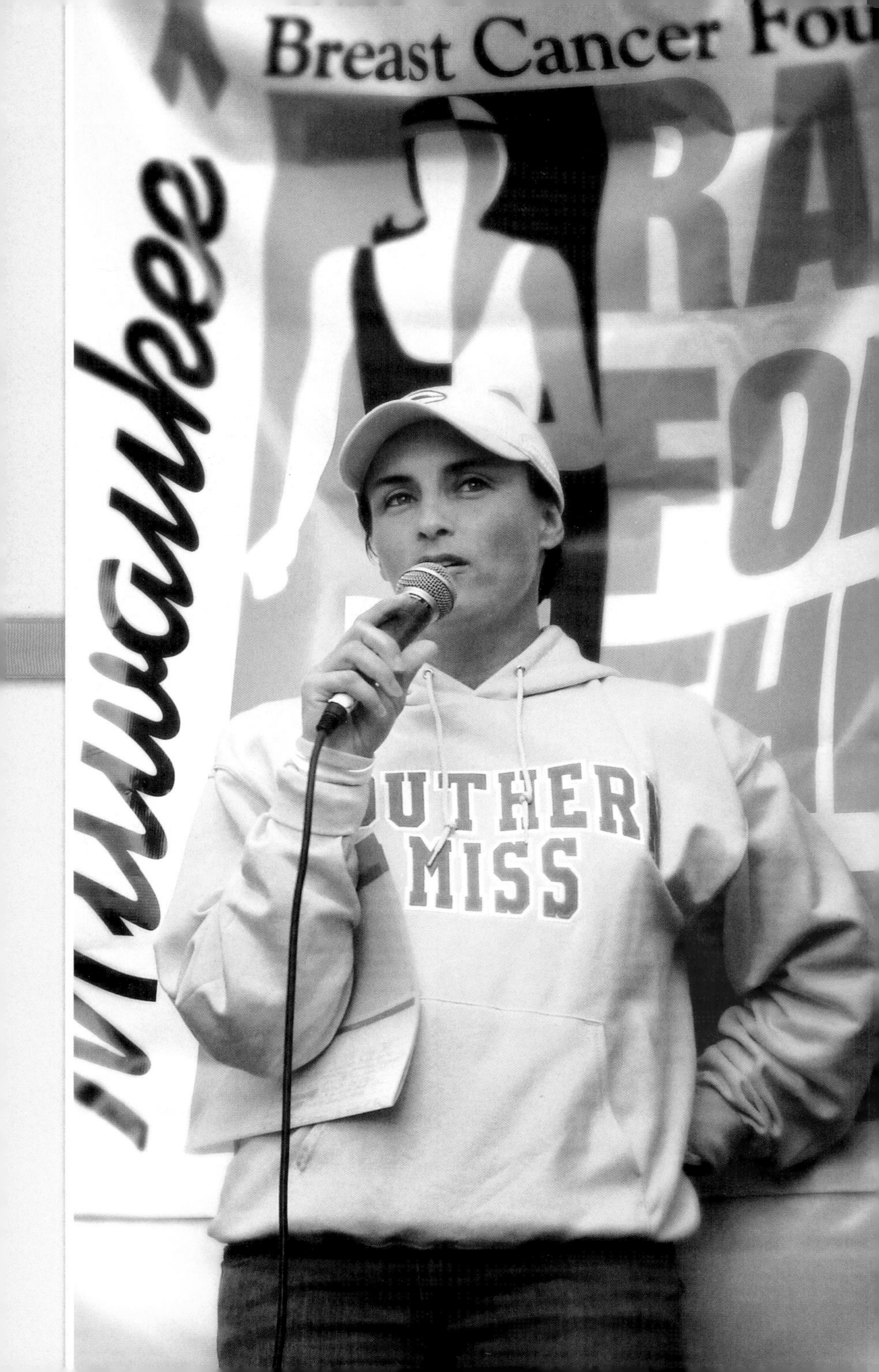
Breast Cancer Fou
SOUTHERN
MISS

← LEFT
Speaking at the
Susan G. Komen
Race for the Cure
event in Milwaukee
2005

Signing one of the pink Packer caps at Race for the Cure, Milwaukee 2005

↑ ABOVE
Breleigh and me signing
pink Packer caps at an
event in Wisconsin
2005

season of Hope

RIGHT →
"Two and a half years later and cancer-free!"
Modeling one of the HOPE Foundation jerseys
April 2007

← LEFT
Brett and me with the girls at "A Night of Faith," a dinner
concert featuring Faith Hill, which raised a lot of money
for women battling breast cancer
2005

RIGHT →
*Brett, the girls, and I walk off the field as a family
at Brett's last home game —or so we thought*
December 21, 2006

*A night out with the girls. Britt, Breleigh,
me, Mom, and Christie.*

2006

Back, from left: Me, Mom, Brittany, John (Brittany's boyfriend), Christie, Josh (Christie's husband), baby Casey
Front: Breleigh, Rocky (Mom's husband)
2006

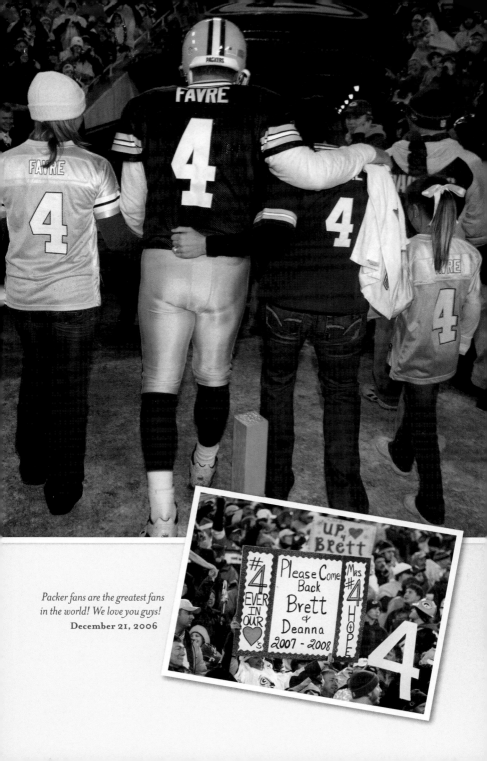

Packer fans are the greatest fans
in the world! We love you guys!

December 21, 2006

Brett always has been and always will be the love of my life
2004

The value of friendship

The only way to cope with the pressures of living on a public stage is to have good friends. When we're in Mississippi, I'm closest to my family and a handful of great friends, but when we're in Green Bay, I rely on our "Green Bay family"—a circle of friends.

I love the story of Lord Byron, the British poet, when he and Robert Peel were schoolmates at Harrow. One day, Byron saw Peel being beaten by a bigger boy. Having no hope of fighting because of his clubfoot, Byron nevertheless went up to the bully and bravely asked how many blows he intended to inflict upon poor Peel.

"What's that to do with you?" roared the bigger boy.

"Because, if you please," replied Byron, trembling. "I would take half."[2]

Coping with public expectation is difficult enough, but I don't know how anyone manages to cope with cancer all by themselves. Not only did I have Brett and my extended family to see me through, but I had friends like Sue Romppanen and Jeannie Pederson. They seemed to have the answers when I needed them, and they helped me stay focused on my Christian walk. I have close friends in my Bible study group, too, but some things are so private that you don't feel comfortable sharing them in a large group.

I don't always feel as knowledgeable as I should be when it comes to the Bible, so I appreciate my group because they help keep me accountable to Bible study. It's also a way to surround myself with people who are positive and uplifting. When I need prayer, I've got a team of prayer warriors. (And I think I always need prayer!)

Angela recently reminded me of what the prophet Daniel went through in Babylon. The king of Babylon had a dream that was so disturbing that he threatened his wise men and counselors with execution unless someone stepped forward to not only interpret the dream, but also to first recount it for the king.

With the threat of certain death hanging over his head, Daniel went to a small circle of friends who shared his faith. "Then Daniel went home and told his friends Hananiah, Mishael, and Azariah what had happened. He urged them to ask the God of heaven to show them his mercy by telling them the secret, so they would not be executed along with the other wise men of Babylon. That night the secret was revealed to Daniel in a vision."[3]

When we are confronted with tough situations, we may be tempted to seek out people with the power to help us—friends with wealth or position or intelligence. But, like Daniel, I have learned the benefit of going to people of faith.

I think most of us have a handful of friends in whom we can confide. My friends in Green Bay helped me cope when I was miles away from my family and friends in Mississippi. If my friends hadn't been there for me, my story would have had a different outcome.

A foundation of family

Brett and I both come from modest homes, and we know what it's like not to be able to get a new pair of shoes or new clothes for an event. Our parents worked hard just to make ends meet.

I was lucky to have great parents, and Brett was, too. He really enjoyed playing football and baseball for his dad. Athletics taught him at an early age to respect his coaches and to practice discipline.

Though neither Brett nor I had a lot of material things while we were growing up, we were rich in that we had loving, hard-working parents who instilled great values in us. My mother has had a huge influence on my life. Even though we had little when I was young, she had a loving and generous heart.

> *Though neither Brett nor I had a lot of material things while we were growing up, we were rich in that we had loving, hard-working parents who instilled great values in us.*

Whenever I'm tempted to lose touch with reality, my family keeps me grounded. They are living examples of what's important in life. When we're in Mississippi, I see them every day, and they keep me humble.

Once Brett and I were married and living in Green Bay, money was no longer a problem for us. We had more than enough to live on and provide for our children, so we wanted to do something for someone else. The difficult part was realizing that we couldn't save the whole world. In 1995, we received so many requests from people in need that we didn't know how to cope with them all. We heard from handicapped people, disease victims, and people with all kinds of financial needs.

One day we were talking with a wise friend, Tom Brosig, who said, "You need a cause to support. Choose a group you want to help, and focus your efforts. You'll never feel like you're accomplishing anything with a shotgun approach."

With that in mind, it didn't take us long to figure out what we wanted to do. Brett's mother used to work with special needs kids at our high school, and Brett always clicked really well with his mother's students.

Everybody especially loved Ronnie Hebert, Irvin's batboy for American Legion baseball, who was mentally handicapped.

Brett really connected with Ronnie, and whenever the team traveled out of town, if they had to spend the night somewhere, Brett roomed with Ronnie.

I went to all of Brett's baseball games in the summer, and Ronnie and I became friends, too. He was several years older, and he'd ride his bike to the park every day. He was always so happy. He'd see me and say, "You're Brett's girlfriend," and he'd hug me, or if he saw me in the bleachers, he'd stick his head out of the dugout, wave, and yell, "Hey, Deanna!"

He stole my heart as well as Brett's.

Jerry West was a special education student in one of Bonita's classes. She signed him up for Irvin's driver's education class. Though Irvin wasn't happy about it at first, he taught Jerry to drive—and Jerry got his license. Now Jerry drives everywhere. He calls us all the time. He'll get on the phone and in one breath he'll say, "Hey, Deanna, how's Brett? How's Breleigh? How's Brittany? How's Bonita? How's Brandi? How's Jeff? How's Scott?" He says it really fast, and he never forgets a single Favre. It's always great hearing from him.

We've known Ronnie and Jerry forever, and friendships like theirs were the motivating force when we created the Brett Favre Fourward Foundation. Brett's foundation benefits disabled and disadvantaged children throughout Mississippi and Wisconsin. We've been blessed with so much, and we needed to give back in some way. What's a better investment than children? We feel they're so important.

Bonita's career in special education was a huge factor in our decision to help disabled children. I was an aide to Bonita in high school, and Brett was always helping his mom with the students. That experience really opened our eyes. When we met kids like Ronnie and Jerry, we began to think about helping others like them.

So many of Bonita's students were not given opportunities

that other children had. The Special Olympics program was the only thing I knew of at the time. A lot of Bonita's students had brothers and sisters that played basketball or softball or went to camp, but the special ed students seemed to get left out.

Bonita thought it was important for her students to have their own activities and their own lives, so she made it a point to take those kids on field trips. She'd take them shopping, to the library, or to the zoo. The school system fought her for years about those trips. They didn't want her to put her students on a bus and take them anywhere. I'm sure the school was concerned about insurance and liability issues, but it just didn't seem fair.

Bonita was determined, though.

She realized that the school was the only place where a lot of her students ever got any special attention, and she wasn't going to take that away from them. Brett and I learned a lot by being around those kids. They were such a joy, and even though they didn't have much, they always seemed so happy. I used to watch Brett with his mom's students, and he always acted like their best friend. I felt like a bride feels when she sees her husband fuss over a new baby.

My mom: an inspiration

Brett has inspired me on many occasions, but my mother has inspired me throughout my life. We didn't have much when I was young, but if Mom had a hundred dollars to spend on us three kids, she'd spend twenty dollars on each of us and give the rest to another family that needed help. She would give her last dollar away if someone knocked on our door and needed groceries. She's never learned how to turn away from someone's need.

I used to think that Mom needed to learn how to say no, but now I can see all the blessings she's gained by being a giving person. I'm so proud of her and so glad she's my mom. I learned a lot about giving from her, and she reminds me of what Jesus said: "It is more blessed to give than to receive."[4]

Jesus talked about giving to others on several occasions. One of his most profound teachings was this: "Don't store up treasures here on earth, where moths eat them and rust destroys them, and where thieves break in and steal. Store your treasures in heaven, where moths and rust cannot destroy, and thieves do not break in and steal. Wherever your treasure is, there the desires of your heart will also be."[5]

Angela recently recommended a book to me by Randy Alcorn called *The Treasure Principle.* In this simple book, he writes that "if we give instead of keep, if we invest in the eternal instead of in the temporal, we store up treasures in heaven that will never stop paying dividends. Whatever treasures we store up on earth will be left behind when we leave. Whatever treasures we store up in heaven will be waiting for us when we arrive."[6]

And how do we "send treasures ahead"? By giving to others. We take what we have been given—by God, who owns the earth and everything in it—and we give to others.

Following my mom's example, every year at Christmastime, I adopt a family and buy gifts for the children. Every year, I get so choked up while shopping for that family—I've had to leave my shopping cart in the middle of the store and go out to the truck to call my mom. I feel so bad for the kids that I'm shopping for, because I wonder what they're going to do the rest of the year.

When I break down, my mom is the person I call, because I know she understands. She has such a humble, compassionate, and giving heart. For years, I've watched her do what she can to help so many people.

Mom's capacity for giving is truly amazing, and she has been a strong Christian role model for me. She has taught me so much over the years, and she is the main reason I am who I am today. My faith, my values, and my desire to help others—all of that comes from her. Her influence on my life is immeasurable, and I have been extremely blessed to have her in my life. I know I am a better mom, a better wife, a better Christian, and a better person for following my mom's example.

Make-A-Wish

Many people don't realize what Brett has done to impact kids' lives. He has worked so hard to get where he is and it perturbs me when people say he hasn't done anything, or when they equate shelling out money with helping other people. You can often be a bigger blessing simply by being there.

One day, Brett came home from practice upset. He sat down and, with tears in his eyes, told me about a little girl named Anna, who had some kind of rare cancer. The Make-A-Wish Foundation had arranged a meeting with her and Brett, and though she was seven years old, Brett said she didn't look much bigger than a toddler. She wasn't going to live much longer, but Brett was so touched by the spirit of life within that child. She was so spunky and sweet and intelligent, and seemed to have the world at her fingertips. Yet she didn't have much time left. "I tried so hard not to cry in front of that

Sometimes the best way to take your mind off your own problems is to help with someone else's.

child," he told me, "and then I looked at Coach Sherman, and he had tears in his eyes, too."

Anna's mother gave Brett a picture of Anna, with her name at the bottom, and Brett put it on our refrigerator, where it stayed the entire season. Every day, we looked at that picture and prayed for Anna and her family. Every time I saw that picture, I couldn't help counting my blessings—I've been blessed with healthy children and a husband who cares about kids.

Sometimes the best way to take your mind off your own problems is to help with someone else's.

The perils of prosperity

For me, the hard part about enjoying material prosperity is seeing my kids grow up with so much. They have no idea what it was like to grow up with very little. I want my girls to appreciate what they have, but how do you instill appreciation in them? Life wasn't easy for Brett and me growing up, but it's easy for Britt and Breleigh. They live in nice houses. They travel. They get to do things most kids never get a chance to do, things Brett and I certainly didn't do when we were young.

Brittany has had her picture taken with Jay Leno, and she has thrown the opening pitch at a professional baseball game. How many kids get to do things like that?

Brett and I have nice homes—one in Mississippi and one in Green Bay—but there are times when we feel guilty about having so much. We tell Brittany how we had only one TV with three channels while we were growing up. Brett will tell the girls about how his family had only one bathroom for six people. And they didn't have a shower until Brett was in seventh or eighth grade. They had a green pot in the bathtub that they used to rinse their hair. When they finally got a shower—in a little bathroom that Irvin and Bonita built just off their bedroom—all the kids stood in line that first night. Scott, Brett, Jeff, and Brandi all wanted to take a shower. It was a big deal. Whenever Brett tells Brittany stories like that, she smiles, but I think she also gets the message.

When Christie, Casey, and I were growing up, everyone had their part to do for the family. In the summer, when school was out and Mom and Dad worked, I was responsible for babysitting my brother and sister and making dinner. I learned how to cook, clean, and do laundry at an early age. It was just what you were supposed to do. We all had chores— Christie's part was to clean the bedroom; mine was to clean the kitchen, etc. Everybody pitched in around the house.

It doesn't seem to work that way anymore with kids—it's like pulling teeth to get them to help around the house. We grew up obeying our parents right away—we knew we'd be in big trouble if we didn't. Of course, we didn't have computers and five hundred TV channels to distract us like kids do today.

Sometimes I worry that Brittany and Breleigh aren't going to be down-to-earth, and that they won't know or care what's going on in the world. That's probably my biggest concern about my children—just making sure they are able to see beyond themselves. I think the foundation helps keep them grounded, because they have an opportunity to see the people we help.

I'm also pretty sure that if Brett hadn't become an NFL quarterback, he'd be a special education teacher and coach in Mississippi. Whenever he visited his mom's classes, he'd give those kids a ton of attention and lots of hugs. Bonita used to tell us, "That's every bit as important, if not more so, than sticking to the lesson plan." If she had a student who loved football, she'd tell him to bring in the scores from Sunday's NFL games. Then she would use the scores to teach that student addition and subtraction. She wanted to make learning fun. She always cared so much. Brett would have been a great special education teacher, too.

When Brett first arrived in Green Bay, he told me about the people he met. One name he mentioned frequently was Leo's. He would tell me about the clowning around they did and how much fun they had together. Finally I asked, "Who's Leo?" I thought he was a teammate. I soon learned that Leo Yelle Jr. worked in the Packers' mail room. He was in his forties and developmentally disabled.

Brett loved going down to the mail room and wrestling with Leo, teasing him, or just hanging out. Brett said they would line up across from each other in a three-point stance, he would call out the signals, and then they'd rush each other. Some of the players told Brett it was nice of him to spend so much time with Leo.

Brett would answer, "It's nice of Leo to cheer me up." Whenever Brett was having a bad day, he would stop in the mail room, and sure enough, Leo would have him laughing in no time. Leo was doing Brett the favor—at least, that's how Brett looked at it.

My husband has the biggest soft spot in the world for kids. He's a kid at heart, so he is very much at ease with them. It's amazing to see him with a Make-A-Wish child. He doesn't care who else is around or what else is going on. He gets on the same level with the child, and you can tell he enjoys talking to him or her.

I've watched while people try to rush him along, and he'll always say, "Go ahead without me if you have to go. I'll be along in a little bit." He truly believes that if we're going to do something, we need to take the time to do it right. He knows that children are smart. If they think we really don't want to be there, we haven't made their wish come true.

In May 1996, we held our first charity golf tournament to kick off the Brett Favre Fourward Foundation's efforts to raise money to provide aid to disadvantaged and disabled children. I was already thinking it would be hectic because it was the first year we'd hosted the tournament, but then it also happened to be the weekend when Brett checked into rehab at the Menninger Clinic. Fortunately, I had a lot of people, such as Tom Brosig, around to help me. With Brett gone, Tom organized the event, and I assisted him and helped host. It was one of the hardest things I've ever had to do. I wanted to crawl into my room, lock the door, and not come out. We had all these celebrities who had agreed to play in the tournament asking, "Where's Brett?" and I had to explain as best I could. We raised $50,000, and I think getting through it made me a stronger person. Now when I see what we're able to do, I'm glad I didn't just crawl into my room and quit.

Heartbreaking needs

The needs are so great that the job of operating a charitable foundation can be frustrating at times. You can't even imagine some of the letters we receive from the charities we help. I always ask that they keep us informed as to what they're doing with the money and what's going on with them. Their feedback really helps and motivates us.

Sometimes it breaks our hearts.

One of the charities we've helped is Hope Haven, a home for battered women and children, located on the Gulf Coast. When I contacted them one time to get an update on two of the children they had taken in after receiving our donation, the letter they sent back brought tears to my eyes.

One of the children, a little girl, was severely malnourished. According to the letter, a doctor from India who had recently come to America stopped at Hope Haven to treat the girl. When the doctor went into the room and saw how bad the situation was, she had to leave to regain her composure. She hadn't thought she would ever see anything like that in America.

I believe a certain responsibility goes along with being an NFL player. You know the biblical saying: "From everyone who has been given much, much will be required."

The other child was a four-year-old girl whose father had been "renting her out" in exchange for drugs. I cried when I read the letter, and then I went home and gave my girls the biggest hugs in the world.

When we hear those kinds of sad, horrible stories, it really affirms what we are doing and makes us want to do even more to help others. We've got to do whatever we can, because so many kids really need our help.

The people who work hands-on with those children have my undying admiration. That kind of work would break my heart. I would try to take them all home, I really would. I could not imagine working at a place like Hope Haven, and I commend those people who, year after year, are still so caring and loving and committed to what they do. I always tell them they are doing something I could never do. Their work is phenomenal.

They usually reply that they couldn't do what I'm doing, either . . . and that's why I think God has me in the right place. Fortunately, we are in a position to use Brett's name to raise money so we can give financial assistance to people who need and deserve it.

When Brett and I visited the Children's Hospital in Milwaukee, we both thought, *That could easily be our child in that bed, and we would want someone to help if they could.*

I believe a certain responsibility goes along with being an NFL player. You know the biblical saying: "From everyone who has been given much, much will be required."[7]

So God may be glorified

I have always believed that we should do good as Jesus commanded in Matthew 6:3-4: "When you give to someone in need, don't let your left hand know what your right hand is doing. Give your gifts in private, and your Father, who sees everything, will reward you."

But one of the hardest things about living in a fishbowl is that people are always eager to report on bad news. They don't always pay attention to positive acts, so sometimes you have to point them out.

We don't want to go around bragging, but after living inside the world of the NFL, I began to realize that sometimes it *is* good to let the world see that football players are doing good things. In Matthew 5:15-16, Jesus also says, "No one lights a lamp and then puts it under a basket. Instead, a lamp is placed on a stand, where it gives light to everyone in the house. In the same way, let your good deeds shine out for all to see, so that everyone will praise your heavenly Father."

Those two verses may sound contradictory, but I've come to realize that Jesus taught that there is a time for doing good in secret, and there is a time for doing good publicly so that God—not the person directly involved—may get the glory.

So that God may get the glory, we let people know where the dollars they contribute to the foundation are going. Some of the groups we support in Mississippi are the Palmer Home for Children; USM's Toy Library and Technology Learning

Center; the Salvation Army; Alpha House Home for Boys; the Frances A. Karnes Center for Gifted Studies; Special Olympics; Association for Retarded Citizens; Make-A-Wish Foundation; Candlelighters Childhood Cancer Foundation (a support group for families of children with cancer); Center for the Prevention of Child Abuse; Mississippi Sheriffs' Boys and Girls Ranches; Caps for Kids; Junior Auxiliary of Gulfport; USM's Children's Center for Communication and Development; Boys and Girls Club of the Gulf Coast; Boys and Girls Club of Hancock County; MHG Development Foundation (which promotes community wellness through Memorial Hospital); Gaits to Success (therapeutic horsemanship for the mentally disabled); and Hope Haven Children's Shelter.

In Wisconsin, we've had the privilege of supporting the Rawhide Boys Ranch; Make-A-Wish Foundation; Special Olympics; CASA of Brown County (which supports abused and neglected children); the "Give a Kid a Book" program; Boys and Girls Clubs of the Fox Valley; United Cerebral Palsy of Wisconsin; the UW–Whitewater program for athletes in wheelchairs; Encompass Early Education and Care; Free S.P.I.R.I.T. Riders (a Fond du Lac, Wisconsin, therapeutic equestrian program for disabled children); Starlight Starbright Children's Foundation (creators of a program that enables sick children to use a private computer network to create an online community of hospitalized children throughout the world); and the Green Bay *Press-Gazette* education program.

For a couple of years, we struggled to find a way to make sure the money we raised was directly benefiting disadvantaged or disabled kids. We didn't want the money to go toward someone's salary or for research—scores of organizations raise money for research. We wanted our organization to touch children's lives directly.

For instance, we once received a letter from a mother who

had two children with muscular dystrophy. She needed to raise money for a van, so we sent her a check. On the other hand, we once received a letter from an older fellow in Milwaukee who wanted to retire but hadn't saved enough money. In essence, he wanted us to fund his retirement account. That's not part of our mission statement, so we passed on that one. We've had letters from people who ask us to pay off their mortgage, fake letters about nonexistent sick children, and people who are just hoping to get Brett's autograph at the bottom of a reply.

We always check out the people who write to us, and I've learned to trust my heart. If the Spirit nudges me after I read a letter, occasionally I'll check into the situation personally. Otherwise, we run everything through the foundation.

We donate two-thirds of all the money we raise, and we invest one-third in the foundation's endowment, which will provide long-term financial stability for the foundation and income for future projects. A lot of charities give away maybe 2 or 3 percent, but we give away the majority of what we take in—isn't that the point of having a charity? Still, we're trying to grow the endowment. Our original goal was to have more than $1 million in the fund by the time Brett retired. I'm pleased to say we've accomplished that, and it's still growing!

I hope our girls will be able to take over the foundation someday. Even if they don't hold events or fund-raisers, I'd still like for them to be able to give away money earned from the endowment.

The foundation's future

Every year, when the *r* word—*retirement*—comes up, I tell Brett the same thing: "I will never tell you to retire. I cannot answer that question for you, and I will never be the reason you retire.

I can give you input, but in your heart, you'll know when you're ready, and you're the only person who will know."

When Brett does decide to retire, I know I'll miss a lot of things about football. I'll miss the camaraderie of it all, the fans, and the excitement of the game. Brett is so enjoyable to watch on the field; you know he's going to do whatever it takes to win or score that touchdown. He's so young at heart, and he's so motivated. I've enjoyed watching him as much as anyone, but I don't enjoy the pounding he takes. Brett has played with bruised ribs, a bruised thigh, a torn muscle in his right side, several sprained ankles, and a broken thumb on his throwing hand. He has coughed up blood on the sidelines. And he's had more close calls than I can count.

Every time I see a lineman get free and go after Brett, my entire body tenses. I'm exhausted after a game; it's almost as if I'd been out on the field myself. I worry and watch and pray that he doesn't get hurt. When he retires, I won't miss that part of the NFL experience.

I will also miss the people of Wisconsin. It's been great to live there during the season. Green Bay is a small town, and we love small towns. The people there are so warm and friendly and supportive of everything we do. We have enjoyed being a part of the community and could not ask for better neighbors. We'll still go back to visit.

I was at a signing last week, and so many people came up to say that they appreciate what we do for the community. I responded by saying that Brett and I appreciate them, as well. It's been a joint effort, and one we have enjoyed very much.

Bart Starr and his wife, Cherry, are terrific examples of what Brett and I would like to become. They haven't lived in Green Bay for years and Bart hasn't played since 1972, but those things don't matter. Packer fans absolutely adore the Starrs because they're wonderful people.

Brett and I have gotten to know the Starrs during our time in Green Bay, and we consider them close friends. They are such role models. They've been through some really tough times, the toughest being the loss of their son Bret in 1988.

I have listened to Bart speak on three or four occasions, and he is a phenomenal motivator. His character and integrity are amazing. I asked him to speak at a student outreach dinner in Hattiesburg one spring, and afterward he and Cherry spent the night at our house.

One of my friends, Stephani, had recently lost her son. She came to breakfast, and over the morning meal she and Cherry began talking about their losses. Afterward, my friend said that her conversation with Cherry was a great comfort.

Every time Bart and Cherry are around, I am reminded of God's ministering angels. I've never met anyone quite like them.

The Starrs say they still feel like part of the Green Bay community, and I think it will be the same way for us. Green Bay has been our home for a long time. I hope it's one place we'll always visit.

Once, as a surprise for Brett, I invited Ronnie Hebert to Green Bay to see a Packer game. It was also the weekend of our foundation dinner, and I wanted Ronnie to be a part of it.

Somehow, I managed to keep the news from my husband. At the dinner, when I brought Ronnie up to the podium, I found myself wishing I'd thought to record the occasion on video. Ronnie talked about how much fun he'd had being Irvin's batboy and getting to go on the American Legion baseball trips. When he talked about Brett being his friend, my big, strong husband had tears in his eyes.

We're connected to a lot of the kids we help. How can we not be?

postgame press

By the time I finished with my chemo and radiation treatments, I knew I wanted to give back to all the people who had given so much to me. Because I'm a professional football player's wife, and because the cameras showed me during a game and the announcer told the world about my breast cancer, I began to receive speaking invitations.

That would've been great—if I were a public speaker. But I'm not. I'm terrified at the thought of speaking in front of people. I had to take a prescription pill before I could even walk up on a stage and accept an award for my husband!

I'm grateful that people want to hear about my struggle with breast cancer, but I can't think of anything I'd feel less comfortable doing than speaking in public. Still, I truly believe that God brought me through breast cancer for a reason, and part of that reason is to help other women.

I told God that if he wanted me to speak so I can help raise money to assist breast cancer patients, and if my story will encourage other women to see a doctor, then he would have to supply me with enough courage to allow me to stand in front of a group.

I truly believe that God brought me through breast cancer for a reason, and part of that reason is to help other women.

I asked my prayer warriors to pray for me before I did a program called *Smart Talk,* which tapes in Milwaukee. I was one of a series of speakers that included Jane Seymour, Patti LaBelle, Debbie Reynolds, and Heather Mills McCartney. I was the speaker for October, which is Breast Cancer Awareness Month.

My dread began to build the minute after I accepted the invitation. On the drive to Milwaukee, I thought I would certainly fall apart on stage, but as I sat in the green room waiting to take the podium, I felt the most amazing calm ease over me. Maybe the Lord knew what he was doing. My friends' prayers were being answered, because I wasn't even trembling.

Then again, I wasn't on stage yet.

I had gone to hear Jane Seymour's talk in June, just to see what I was in for. She was so polished, so professional, that I found myself believing there was no way I was going to be able to get through my segment as smoothly as she did. I wasn't a famous actress; I didn't have parents who took me to stage plays and art classes while I was growing up. Jane Seymour grew up in a cultured climate; I grew up playing basketball.

While listening to Jane speak, I sank deeper into my chair, absolutely positive that nothing I could say would impress anybody. Then the man next to me leaned over and whispered, "You know, you're going to captivate your audience because people are going to be able to relate to you."

He must have been reading my mind.

I straightened up my posture as the truth of his words sank in. I'm an average person. Most people think of my husband as a celebrity, but I don't, because I knew him when he was a kid just like me. We're regular people, so if people can be touched by an ordinary woman . . .

When my turn came in October, I stood before the audience and told my story without trembling or going blank or having a panic attack. Afterward, I heard from dozens of people who were touched by something I'd said. Time after time, they told me they could relate to my struggles and my heartaches.

I began to see how God could use even my cancer to bring glory to his name.

That's when I began to see how God could use even my cancer to bring glory to his name. You can give to people and put Bibles in their hands, but it's not until they hear stories of how God can work in a regular person's life that they begin to understand.

He can work in their lives, too.

I'm the same as a lot of people. If you're going to teach me something, I need to see an example of the finished product. So now I think of myself as a product—maybe not *quite* finished—that can demonstrate how God can work in someone's life.

The positives of suffering

I've often heard people say, "If God brings you *to* it, he'll bring you *through* it." I believe that with all my heart. When I stand to speak in front of a group, I know I'm not there because it's my profession or my talent. I'm there because it's what God has called me to do. I'm not a gifted speaker. I struggle with nerves every time.

But God uses me. And that's an amazing thing.

Tough situations can make you a stronger person, and the way you handle all the things that happen in your life can actually build character. I think I'm a better person because of my struggles, and I know I'm stronger than I used to be.

One lesson I've learned is that tragedy and illness put life in perspective. In the light of a crisis, little things don't matter so much.

For those of us who believe in Christ, our primary goals are glorifying God and getting to heaven. That's what matters. That way, when we lose someone we love, we know we'll see that person again. All the nonsense we bring into our lives by surrounding ourselves with the wrong people or by being in groups that are gossipy—those things are so petty and irrelevant.

When other people see bad things happen to my family, they realize there really is no perfect life. Sometimes there are no happy endings. Bad things happen to everyone; no one is immune to tragedy or cancer or death. When these things happen, we have to take our situation and turn it into something positive.

When Brett's dad died, I hoped there were fathers and sons watching the tribute game who would realize that life is short and they need to spend more time together.

And losing Casey . . . my brother and I had a rough relationship for a while, but now I'm able to tell people, "Never have so much pride that you can't reach out and say that you love someone." Whatever trials come into your life, you have to learn from them and try to see them from a positive perspective.

If my cancer results in opportunities to inspire other women, or help them financially, then that is a good thing.

We are always quick to turn to God when something

tragic comes along. Obviously, I used to do that, too. But now I also try to be thankful for all the good things that happen in my life and all the opportunities that God has sent my way. I

BREAST CANCER *detection and prevention*

Many people assume that a family history of breast cancer is a woman's number one risk factor, but at thirty-five, I had breast cancer and no family history of the disease. Researchers tell us that a woman's susceptibility to cancer involves her age, immune status, nutritional habits, genetics, and ethnicity. Only 5 percent of all cancers in the United States are thought to be attributable to heredity.[1]

As we learn more about cancer, more doctors are placing an emphasis on prevention through healthy living. A low-fat, high-fiber diet that includes a variety of fruits and vegetables is recommended, as is daily exercise.

Newsweek recently reported that regular exercise also benefits women who have already had breast cancer. Two-thirds of all breast cancers are considered estrogen receptor positive (that is, the hormone estrogen fuels their growth), and regular exercise appears to lower the amount of estrogen in the bloodstream. Exercise also burns fat, and fat manufactures a substance called aromatase, which converts other hormones into estrogen.

After tracking nearly three thousand breast cancer patients for up to fourteen years, researchers found that recurrence rates and deaths from breast cancer (and from other causes) dipped 26 to 40 percent among those who exercised most. Furthermore, you don't have to be a weight lifter or marathoner to get this protective benefit—brisk walking for three to five hours a week—about thirty minutes a day—resulted in the biggest benefits. Even being active for one hour a week reduced the patients' risks.[2]

Do your family and friends a favor—learn to make time for exercise, and pick up some fresh fruit and veggies at the grocery store. You may not only live longer, but you'll be a better manager of the body God has given you.

know that every good thing comes from God, and I've grown so much by realizing that I need to be grateful for those good things. I think a thankful heart helps to establish an ongoing relationship with God, so that he's not just someone I turn to when I'm going through a rough time. He's always there, every day. It's exciting to realize that I need him not only in the bad times, but in every hour. That's how my faith has grown. I've seen good things happen, good people have come into my life, and I've been able to help people—those are all blessings from God.

I'm not an overly emotional person, and I'm pretty even-keeled, but when I talk about my experiences, I often get choked up. Interestingly, it rarely happens twice at the same place in the story. Sometimes I wonder if someone in the audience needs to be touched in a certain way, and my unplanned and unexpected tears are what God uses to reach their heart.

I have learned that I must depend on God to do the things I can't do on my own. I used to be so proud of my independence; now I'm grateful for my dependence on God. He gave Brett and me the strength to get through some tough days, and he gave Brett the strength to make a positive change in his life. He brought me through chemo, and now he is giving me the courage to speak to women who need to hear about breast cancer.

I used to be so proud of my independence; now I'm grateful for my dependence on God.

Before I speak, I always go into a quiet corner to pray, "God, I'm here for you. Lord, let me be a reflection of you. I don't want to be a hero; I don't want people to say that I'm awesome. I want them to see you, Father. I want them to glorify you."

In mid-May 2005, when I had just a tiny bit of hair on my head, I drove down to a broadcast station to record what I *thought* was a radio spot. When I arrived at the station, however, I discovered that I'd been scheduled for a TV spot. I'd shown up without a wig or a decent application of makeup. And they wanted to take *pictures*.

They had a girl dab some makeup on my face, but I couldn't do anything about my bare head. I was a little nervous about having my picture taken with hardly any hair. I hadn't sat for any photos since beginning my chemo, and I would have been happy to wait another year before I walked within twenty feet of a camera.

And then I thought of all the women who are going through cancer treatments and have proudly gone out in public without their wigs. Most women wear their wigs until their hair grows out to a certain length, but many brave women have the courage to appear bareheaded in order to make a statement.

So I allowed myself to be photographed with my "spiky" look. I was told that the pictures would be used as posters to promote an upcoming breast cancer walk. *Posters!* Not just a little photograph buried in a magazine somewhere. Then, in the following weeks, several women came up to me and told me how that particular poster touched their lives. "You really looked beautiful," one woman told me, "and when I saw that you had the courage to go out with such short hair, you gave me the courage to take off my wig, too."

Their stories always made me feel great, but those women probably helped me far more than I helped them. Their encouragement has kept me going and lets me know that I am doing the right thing when I share my story.

When I went to the local Susan G. Komen Race for the Cure in Milwaukee the year after my treatment, more than nine thousand people showed up, a 70 percent increase over the previous year. I'm not sure why the crowd was so much bigger, but I'd like to think that the public efforts of cancer patients like me have helped to erase the stigma and have encouraged others to get out and work to find a cure for breast cancer.

Friends inspire me

I have a heart for helping women because so many women have helped me—and many of them may not even know how they've inspired me. My female friends comfort, help, and encourage me every day through their example, their friendship, and their prayers.

Though my mom has definitely had the greatest influence on my life, there is no doubt that my closest female friend is my sister, Christie. We share and know everything about each other. We have no secrets between us, but there are a couple of things we've never told our husbands.

One day Christie and I went to Wal-Mart together. I don't remember what we were looking for, but we put our purses in a shopping cart and pretty much wandered all over the store.

A few minutes after we left the garden department and went back into the main part of the store, we realized that our purses were missing. I panicked—my car keys were gone, along with my wallet, and Christie's, too. Christie ran to the parking lot and told a security guard that our purses were gone, while I backtracked and tried to figure out where someone could have taken them.

A few minutes later, the security guard and Christie came to join me. He was telling her that it's really not safe to leave your purse in the cart, but he'd called the police and they'd try to find our purses. I called Brett, told him what happened, and asked him to bring the extra car key so I could drive home. Meanwhile, Christie gave descriptions of our purses to the security guard, who stationed employees by the door in case someone tried to walk out with our handbags.

I met Brett outside, got the extra key, and went back inside the store to find Christie. I couldn't believe what had happened—our bags were in the cart, and then, nothing! I felt sick to my stomach.

While Christie and the security guard monitored the front door, I wandered through the store, trying to retrace our steps. I went through the sliding door that led to the garden area, and felt my heart do a double beat when I looked up and saw a shopping cart in the aisle—with our purses safely inside.

Somehow, we'd been distracted while talking and walked away with the wrong cart.

I grabbed the cart with the handbags and hurried to the front of the store. I thanked the security guard for all his help and told him I'd found our purses, and then Christie and I hurried outside.

To this day, we have never told our husbands that we were ditzy enough to have walked off with the wrong cart.

Christie and I laugh together all the time. We can look at each other, realize what the other is thinking, and burst out in a laugh. When my family's in Green Bay, Christie and I call each other at least every other day. We're best friends and sisters, but our relationship goes even deeper than that. There's a bond between us and our mom that doesn't exist anywhere else.

Another woman who has been a particular inspiration to our family is June Mommaerts, aka "June Bug." She is my definition of a hero! She lost her husband to cancer when her youngest child was two and her oldest sixteen. "Miss June," as our family knows her, worked and raised her five children to be fine, successful adults. While she was raising those children as a single mother, she was diagnosed with breast cancer.

As someone who's had cancer and has been a single mother, I don't know how she managed both at the same time. Miss June has always been one of my heroes, because after her diagnosis, she didn't have a pity party. Her attitude has always been, "These are the cards I've been dealt, so I'll play this hand and get through it."

Miss June has helped me take care of my children for years, and my girls always look forward to seeing her when we go back to Green Bay. The first thing Breleigh wants to do when we pull into Green Bay is call Miss June.

I adore her attitude—she never complains and she never asks why. She simply does whatever has to be done. Whenever I have a task ahead that I think is hard—especially if it involves public speaking—I draw strength from and find inspiration in women like Miss June.

A foundation of giving

I know that I'm fortunate because our family has good medical insurance. When my cancer was diagnosed, I didn't have to worry about choosing between paying for a noncovered treatment or making the mortgage payment. But not everyone qualifies for insurance, and not everyone can afford it. I'd like to see fair treatment across the board, with every patient getting the best care possible.

During my treatment, as I sat in the clinic waiting room and looked around, I wondered about my fellow patients. The older woman in the scarf by the window—was she covered by insurance, eligible for Medicare, or paying for her treatments out of her pocket? Would she be sitting in the chemo chair for two hours or eight?

When one of my medical bills arrived, I skimmed through the list of charges and couldn't believe that a single Neulasta shot cost more than $3,000—and patients are supposed to have one of those after every chemo treatment. I showed the statement to Brett, and he whistled in disbelief. How can people without insurance afford those kinds of expenses?

If I had been diagnosed with cancer when I was a single mom, I wouldn't have been able to afford the excellent medical care I received.

Brett and I have indeed been blessed in recent years, but I have keen memories of my days as a single mother. I bounced checks not because I was a lousy bookkeeper, but because there simply wasn't enough money to cover all my bills. If I had been diagnosed with cancer when I was a single mom, I wouldn't have been able to afford the excellent medical care I received.

The average hospital bill for treating breast cancer was $17,200 in 2003, but that only refers to patients who received care in a *hospital*.[3] The number of hospitalizations for breast cancer treatment is declining because more women are choosing to be treated at outpatient facilities.

Based on information from a large health maintenance organization, the U.S. Congressional Budget Office estimated that in the first year after diagnosis, the average breast cancer patient will spend about $20,000 on treatments.[4]

I don't know about you, but when I was a single mother, I didn't have an extra twenty grand in the bank.

I thought about other women who are single and working a job during their chemo treatments. What if they're too sick to go into work? How can they afford their medical bills if they're paid by the hour and can't work? How do they do it?

I wanted to help women in that situation, but I wasn't sure how to begin.

The HOPE Foundation

After my breast cancer became public knowledge, I began to get requests to speak, along with generous honorariums for speaking. I also began to receive money from people making donations to Brett's foundation because their mother or sister had breast cancer.

I wished there was a way I could pass that money along to women who were financially strapped and suffering from breast cancer. Because I'd been a single parent without health insurance, I knew what a little extra money could mean to others in that situation.

So, with Brett's support, I established the Deanna Favre HOPE Foundation. Like the Brett Favre Fourward Foundation, the HOPE Foundation is a 501(c)(3) organization. Contributions are fully tax-deductible.

Establishing a foundation is quite an enterprise, requiring mountains of paperwork and a small army of lawyers. We've also had to clarify our vision for this project so that we're not throwing money blindly at a problem. We want our donations to make a direct impact on the lives of specific women, rather than going to someone's salary. Lots of organizations donate money for research; that's why we focus specifically on helping women who are struggling to pay medical bills and still somehow put dinner on the table.

People have been very generous with their support. We've received financial gifts from individuals as well as checks from wedding parties—couples who sent out invitations with a note reading, "In lieu of gifts, please send a donation in our honor to the HOPE Foundation."

The HOPE Foundation raises money by selling tote bags, sweatshirts, ball caps, and other items through our Web site: www.DeannaFavre4Hope.com. All profits go to the foundation for distribution to breast cancer patients. In 2005, when we began to sell pink Packer caps on our Web site, they outsold regular Packer caps during the first half of the year![5]

The Packers were selling pink caps before I was diagnosed with breast cancer, but after my diagnosis was made public, sales really took off. In all, the Packers Pro Shop sold more than 200,000 pink caps, raising $1.2 million, which was divided among twelve charities statewide.[6] The HOPE Foundation was one of the twelve.

Some of the money from the Pro Shop cap sales went to the Marshfield Clinic's mobile mammogram clinic, a vehicle that is almost continually booked. The program intends to buy a second unit to reach more women and help with the detection and prevention of breast cancer.

I've been asked how I feel when I go to Packer games and see a sea of pink hats. Some people interpret it as a show of support specifically for me and my family, but I think it represents something much broader. I think it simply shows how many families have been touched by breast cancer.

Last year, the HOPE Foundation gave $3,000 gifts to twelve people who qualified under our mission statement. We sent them each a check they could use for their medical bills or to buy groceries. When I was a single mother, I know I would have appreciated having the freedom to spend the gift on my most pressing needs. We hope to continue to grow, and to help even more women in the upcoming year.

We hear from so many women in Wisconsin and

Mississippi—women who have three kids at home and who have to be off work while they go through chemotherapy. Women whose husbands abandoned them after a breast cancer diagnosis. Women who have no insurance and no way to buy shoes for their children.

That's when I take great joy in writing a check and making sure it goes directly to one of these families in need. I always ask them to drop us a note to let us know how they're doing. Sometimes I run into these people later and they tell me how grateful they were to get some help while they were going through their treatment.

I believe the greatest good we accomplish is providing these women with hope—and that's why we call it the HOPE Foundation. When a woman is going through breast cancer treatment, especially as a single mom, it's easy to feel hopeless. She feels alone, with no one to help her or provide a source of hope. Our job is to give these women hope, faith, and strength, and to show them they are not alone.

I wish I could personally introduce you to some of the incredibly brave women I've met through the HOPE Foundation. Because that's impossible, I thought I'd share, with their permission, a couple of the wonderful letters we have received.

Dear Deanna,

I want to thank you for your generous grant that my good friend, Charlene, surprised me with recently. I don't think I've ever been so surprised and so honored.

When I first got diagnosed with breast cancer and realized I would not be working, I knew that I could not deal with cancer and financial worries at the same time. It was too big for me, so I gave it to God and asked Him to please take care of me and my husband. I know your foundation's generosity is God's way of doing just that.

My hope is that your foundation continues to prosper and change women's lives. May God bless you and your family.

Sincerely,
Leigh Ann Kemp

JUNE 8, 2007

Dear Deanna,

Thank you for your time in reading my letter.
I just wanted to tell you that I keep you in
my prayers for continued good health and for
continued strength to fight this disease of breast
cancer. I also pray for your continued strength
in your personal battle against it. The personal
anguish and worry of the disease is overwhelming,
especially as a wife and mother. We pray to see
and enjoy retirement, and to see our children
and grandchildren grow up.

Thank you for bringing strength to me. For
being the perfect example of strength and class
to handle your diagnosis, treatment, and survival
as you have.

I first met you in November of 2004. I met
you and Brett entering St. Vincent Hospital for
one of your first treatments. I am an emergency
nurse there and I had just wheeled a discharged
patient out to the Webster Avenue entrance.
I was very surprised to see you; I think my heart
actually fluttered. Brett was a few steps behind.
It didn't take me long to see the serious looks
on your faces, the fear in your eyes. I immediately

(continued)

wanted to hug you, wish you the very best, and give you the cheerleader-in-me pep talk that you would do just fine. Instead, I chose to protect your privacy and confidentiality. I took a deep breath, and whispered to myself, "God bless you, Deanna—you can do it! Stay strong!"

To this day, I don't know if I did the right thing. I wanted so much to give you a hug for strength and encouragement. If my memory serves me correctly, a few weeks later I remember praying, "Dear God, please let Deanna have a nice Thanksgiving. Please don't let her be sick from the chemo on Thanksgiving."

Nine months later, as I waited for my own biopsy results, I remember telling my husband, Darrell, "If Deanna Favre can have cancer, anyone can"—and I did. I was diagnosed in August 2005, followed by surgery, chemo, and radiation. A little over two months after treatment—last year, 2006—I did the Bellin Run—my first one ever. It was wonderful. Every step of the way, I remembered all the days I'd spent in bed and all the people who supported me during my treatment. I was so grateful to be upright and moving. It was wonderful having my strength back. My first chemo was pretty rough—

(continued)

I spent eight days in bed—I only got up to go to the bathroom, so for me to do the Bellin Run was quite the feat—no pun intended. My middle son, Max, ran also; he finished ahead of me and came back to cheer me on—it was priceless. I finished with tears in my eyes. My boys, Alex (now 13), Maxwell (11), and Dexter (7), along with my husband, Darrell, gave me great strength. They totally supported me, as did my mom, dad, sister, and in-laws. My co-workers at St. Vincent Emergency Department were also family to me. I was so lucky to have such wonderful support.

So, Deanna—thank you for all you have done to support those affected by breast cancer; for being a pillar of strength; and for turning such a horrible challenge in your life into a positive outcome, enriching the lives of others, and so generously giving of yourself. God bless you in your efforts.

May you stay cancer free, and may you get stronger each day of your survival. Please don't let worry overwhelm you. May all your energy go toward continued health, love for your family, and into fighting this disease.

I am blessed to have three wonderful boys— Alex, Maxwell, and Dexter. Each has an x in his

(continued)

name, for when Mom and Dad are gone, they are each left with a "kiss" in their names. Thanks to people like you, I hope to see them grow up, despite the diagnosis of breast cancer. God bless you and your family.

Love,
Carol Mijal

Also—one of my most prized possessions from my cancer diagnosis is an autographed pink Packer hat, signed by you and Brett. It was given to me by a wonderful person and nurse by the name of Connie Worzala, cancer coordinator at St. Vincent Hospital. It was a tremendous token of strength to get me through a difficult time.

As the mother of three boys, I always laughed about how we didn't have any pink in our house. Wow, did that ever change after my diagnosis! Along came pink flowers, pink Packer hats, pink blankets, pink bracelets, pink cards, and pink art projects from school. Alex even cut a cancer ribbon in our grass. Yes, my boys are tough enough to wear pink!

My best to you!

We're in this struggle together

In June 2007, I competed in my first 10K race, the Bellin Run in Green Bay. My goal was to finish in under an hour, which I did with a time of 59:52. I was thrilled, not only because I had reached a personal goal, but also because I received a $15,000 check after the race, made out to the HOPE Foundation. The organizers of the Bellin Run made the contribution to support breast cancer education and to provide state-of-the-art breast imaging and diagnostic services for women.[7]

Someday, I pray the HOPE Foundation raises enough money to establish an endowment fund; that way there will always be money available to help women in need. I know that's a big goal and a big challenge, but I would love to see it happen. Right now, we are helping women only in Mississippi and Wisconsin, but I'd love to see us grow large enough to help women across the nation. We'd also like to provide hope through a comprehensive Web site where women could go for information to educate and encourage them as they work to overcome breast cancer.

Some of the proceeds from this book are going to the HOPE Foundation and the cancer patients we serve. By buying this book, I hope you'll not only gain good information, but will also be blessed by taking part in helping other women in a tangible way.

I see this book, and everything associated with it, as yet another way God has provided to help me bring good out of a period of suffering. As it says in the book of Romans, "We know that God causes everything to work together for the good of those who love God and are called according to his purpose for them."[8]

And you know what? When I think about the things I've sacrificed for the life I now lead—my dietetics program, for instance—I realize that the work I've done with Brett is probably more rewarding than anything I could have done with a graduate degree. It would have been hard for me to work as a dietitian while living six months in one state and six months in another. What has worked out—running the foundations—has become a career for me. I understand the work, and I get a lot of satisfaction out of writing checks to charities and knowing that specific women and children are getting the help they need.

I haven't made a ton of money for myself, but I've helped raise money for charities. Making money for yourself might be satisfying for some people, but I'd rather give it away. That's where the real satisfaction comes from.

God has bountifully provided for us. Brett has done well, he's been blessed and gifted, and I don't need to make money to support the family. I enjoy what I do, and I consider my charity work a real blessing from God.

winner's trophy

CHAPTER THIRTEEN

I have refined you, but not as silver is refined.
Rather, I have refined you in the furnace of suffering.
I will rescue you for my sake—yes, for my own sake!

ISAIAH 48:10-11

When I finished my last radiation treatment and heard my doctor say that the cancer had been eradicated, I faced a different world. I had assumed that when it was all over, I would slip back into my life's comfortable rhythm and purpose as if nothing had ever happened. But the very fabric of my existence had forever been changed.

After cancer, I looked at the world through different eyes. Big things that once seemed so important now seemed trivial; little things that once seemed trivial now seemed incredibly precious. Something as simple as being able to get out of bed, get dressed, and drive my daughter to school was a cause for celebration. Sitting with Brett on the sofa, feeling his arm holding me tight—these are things I will never again take for granted. Things I used to hurry through—like cooking breakfast for my girls—are now things I treasure.

Big things that once seemed so important now seemed trivial; little things that once seemed trivial now seemed incredibly precious.

One night we were all together watching a movie in the den. Brett and I were on the sofa, Brittany was in a chair, and Breleigh was on the ottoman. Instead of watching the movie, I found myself staring at Breleigh—she had a faraway look in her eyes, and it was obvious she was deep in thought about something.

After a few minutes, she turned to me. "What are you thinking about?" I asked.

"What?"

"Weren't you thinking about something?"

She smiled. "Yeah, how did you know?"

"I could just tell."

Simply watching your children *live*—paying attention to what they're doing—is an incredible blessing. For me, that moment in the den was bigger than any being-on-television moment could ever be. It feels good to sit back and watch your family, and to be a part of the different things going on in their lives. Moments like that are my priority now.

Ironically, just as I wanted to settle down and enjoy my family to the fullest, requests for personal appearances began flooding in. Brett has always gotten dozens of invitations each month; now people wanted to hear from me as well. As much as I wanted to be able to help, I knew I couldn't accept every invitation. Cancer had caused me to take a new look at my life. I wanted to dedicate myself to my priorities.

In one of her devotional books, Joyce Meyer says, "Say no to the good and yes to the great." That little snippet of advice gave me the freedom to be able to say no—something a lot of women find difficult. As mothers and wives, we are accustomed to being caretakers, and we want to make everyone happy. But there aren't enough hours in the day to do everything and still reserve time for family, friends, and a personal relationship with God.

When I sort through letters requesting a personal appearance, some touch me more than others (for whatever reason), and I find myself led to do certain ones. But most of the time, I end up saying, "This is really good work you're doing, but I'll have to decline the invitation because the volume of requests is so great."

A new appreciation

Part of the silver lining in the cloud of cancer is the way a husband and wife begin to appreciate each other. I suppose it's human nature to treasure something you could have lost, and that's been true in my relationship with Brett. I love our quiet, comfortable times at home, when we can relax and be ourselves.

For his part, Brett has become much more attentive. My illness forced him to learn how to be a more supportive husband, and I think it was good for him to sit beside me as I received my first chemo treatment. For so many years, I supported him; maybe it was time for us to exchange roles.

While I was undergoing my treatments, for the first time Brett blew me a kiss from the football field.

Last spring, we went to Disney World. I was standing and talking to some friends when Brett picked a flower, gave it to Breleigh, and said, "Take this to your mom and tell her I love her."

I don't know about your husband, but most of the men my

husband knows aren't likely to do things like that when other people are watching. Brett has changed, and my cancer is part of the reason. That, and everything we've gone through together over the years.

We have both grown up a lot through the tragedies that have struck our lives. Brett once told a reporter about how our lives have changed: "Me and Deanna have always been athletic, outgoing, immune from everything. But in the matter

SURVIVING *breast cancer*

Some people believe you are as good as dead the moment you receive a cancer diagnosis, but nothing could be further from the truth. According to the American Cancer Society, the percentage of people living five years after a diagnosis of any type of cancer shot up to 66 percent with a diagnosis after 1995 and is continuing to rise. For breast cancer patients, the five-year survival numbers rose from 75 percent in the 1970s to nearly 90 percent by 2002.[1]

Part of the increase in survival rates comes from a major adjustment in researchers' thinking. Instead of attempting to completely eradicate some cancers, doctors are looking for ways to corral and disable malignant cells. "There was a mind shift that happened in the 1980s," says Dr. John Glaspy, professor of medicine at UCLA's Jonsson Comprehensive Cancer Center. "We realized that there is a power in the chronic-disease model where you can focus on a high quality of living with a disease instead of necessarily curing it. If we can have people alive, productive, and happy, that's now viewed as a very wonderful outcome."[2]

Right now, doctors have a large arsenal of drugs to combat breast cancer—more than any other type of cancer. By using "smart drugs," they are able to prevent cancer cells from dividing and growing. Newer drugs are being developed so quickly that Dr. Daniel Hayes, clinical director of the breast oncology program of a year, everything happened to us. I'm thirty-six, but I have to admit that I felt still, for the most part, like I was fifteen years old. And Deanna and I'd been dating since I was fourteen. I still look at her as the girl I was chasing around in ninth grade. And when Dad passed away and her brother passed away and she got cancer, you go, 'What happened?' We're still kids. Kids are not supposed to get cancer. Kids are not supposed to see their younger brother get killed."[7]

at the University of Michigan Comprehensive Cancer Center, says, "It's fun to be an oncologist right now."[3]

"Most women who get treated for breast cancer will not have a recurrence," Dr. JoAnne Zujewski of the National Cancer Institute told *Newsweek* magazine. "We have excellent treatments that are getting better all the time. Mortality is down."[4]

More specifically, women with early-stage breast cancer who choose lumpectomy with radiation therapy live just as long as those who chose mastectomy. After twelve years, only one out of approximately ten women who had lumpectomy/radiation will have had a recurrence of cancer in the same breast.[5]

As of June 2002, the five-year survival rate for all women with breast cancer (including advanced cases) is 86 percent. Women with cancer that has not metastasized (spread to the lymph system or other parts of the body) have a five-year survival rate of 96 percent.[6]

Improvements in the detection of breast cancer and advances in treatment have led to a huge improvement in survival rates. That's why it's important for you to do a monthly self-exam and have any suspicious lumps examined by a doctor.

Don't be afraid. The future for breast cancer patients is brighter than it has ever been. ஃ

No doubt about it, tragedy has matured us. We don't think of ourselves as kids anymore.

A HealthLink article from the Medical College of Wisconsin reported on a study of communication between cancer patients and their spouses. Researchers weren't surprised to find that patients and spouses communicated. They *were* surprised to discover that "almost to a person, husbands and wives reported undergoing personality changes" that had taken them "to a different and enhanced level of meaning in their lives."[8]

> *No doubt about it, tragedy has matured us. We don't think of ourselves as kids anymore.*

Marc Silver, writing in *U.S. News and World Report,* says that "in the world of cancer, people talk about the New Normal—a different sort of life, changed (for the better, one hopes) by the brush with death."[9]

After his wife's mastectomy and fourteen weeks of tough chemo, Frank Sadowski, a vice president at Amazon.com, told Silver, "Cancer certainly isn't a gift, but it's a blessing. As crazy as that sounds coming out of my mouth, I think, in a way, it has been a blessing for my wife, and for both of us in different ways. It has really changed her outlook on life."[10]

About his own response to his wife's cancer, Frank says, "There's been a significant change in the way I prioritize things and what I think is important. Things that used to be really, really important . . . aren't important in the same way. Life's too short to mess around with this stuff."[11]

My New Normal is a richer, fuller world. I have learned to appreciate the incomparable value of things like these:

- A quiet night
- Friends who accept you when you're at your worst

- Someone else making dinner
- A full night's sleep
- Watching your children live
- Running errands without feeling like you're running a marathon
- Giving to others
- The warmth of a family hug
- A beautiful day of sunshine
- A rainy day with puddles
- Cold, bitter snow
- Celebrating another holiday, knowing it won't be your last

I have learned that all of us have struggles—it might be a disease, a bad relationship, abuse, alcohol, or the loss of a loved one. Tragedy does not discriminate, and no one will live a trouble-free life.

In his classic *My Utmost for His Highest*, Oswald Chambers writes:

> *An average view of the Christian life is that it means deliverance from trouble. It is deliverance **in** trouble, which is very different. . . . If you are a child of God, there certainly will be troubles to meet, but Jesus says do not be surprised when they come. . . .*
>
> *God does not give us overcoming life: He gives us life as we overcome. The strain is the strength. If there is no strain, there is no strength. Are you asking God to give you life and liberty and joy? He cannot, unless you will accept the strain. Immediately you face the strain, you will get the strength. . . .*
>
> *God never gives strength for tomorrow, or for the next hour, but only for the strain of the minute.*[12]

I have learned that during my darkest moments, I am never alone, for God is always with me. When I let him help me, my path is smoothed and my spirit is calmed. And he has blessed me with family and friends who give me the strength to survive whatever trials may come.

I have learned that God can use all things for good—even my personal heartaches—if I will let him.

I have learned that you should never take anyone for granted, or miss the opportunity to say how much you love them.

I have learned that life is a journey, but the road does not always take you where you think you should go. There are twists and turns on the highway of life; there are roadblocks and forks that require you to make tough decisions. But no matter where the road may take you, God will go with you and guide you.

I have learned to cherish three words:

Faith . . . that God has an ultimate and good plan for my life.

Hope . . . for my children, my marriage, and my future.

Love . . . for my family and friends, a blessing I will never take for granted.

faith for the future

Faith is the confidence that what we hope for will actually happen; it gives us assurance about things we cannot see.

HEBREWS 11:1

What happened to poor, suffering Job? After losing his wealth, his children, and his health, did he curl up and die?

Not by a long shot. Job sat in ashes and painful misery while his friends came to visit him. After considering the wretched state of Job's life, his friends spent several days trying to convince him that he must have done something awful, something that deserved the wrath of God.

Poor Job kept insisting that he hadn't done anything. "Let the Almighty answer me," he said. "Let my accuser write out the charges against me. I would face the accusation proudly. I would wear it like a crown. For I would tell him exactly what I have done. I would come before him like a prince."[1]

Later, faced with Job's pride and overconfidence, God

reminded him of who was the Creator and who was the creature. Job humbly replied, "I was talking about things I knew nothing about, things far too wonderful for me. . . . I take back everything I said, and I sit in dust and ashes to show my repentance."[2]

Seeing the humble state of Job's heart, God restored his fortunes, giving him twice as much as before. "So the LORD blessed Job in the second half of his life even more than in the beginning. . . . He also gave Job seven more sons and three more daughters. . . . Job lived 140 years after that, living to see four generations of his children and grandchildren. Then he died, an old man who had lived a long, full life."[3]

Through his experience with suffering, Job learned several good lessons:

It's not wise to question God's motives.

God operates in ways we don't always understand.

God is trustworthy. Though we may pass through a season of suffering, the end result is joy.

Keeping faith

I'll be honest—sometimes it's hard to live like a Christian in a world of wealth and privilege. That's why I'm always grateful for our Mississippi roots. Whenever I'm tempted to think we *deserve* to fly on a private jet, I just remember our upbringing and realize how fortunate we are. God has blessed us with material prosperity, but he's also given us some unique responsibilities.

Some people assume that all professional athletes behave like spoiled rich kids, but that's not true. There are hundreds of Christians in the NFL, and I've really been impressed by some of the younger guys who aren't at all into the party lifestyle.

The late Reggie White, number 92 for the Packers,

always impressed me with his consistent stand for Christ. Once, Reggie found himself at the center of what could have been quite a controversy over postgame prayers in the center of the field.

The practice of praying at midfield began in 1990 when eight players from the New York Giants and San Francisco 49ers gathered and knelt to pray after the game. Many fans aren't even aware of the practice. The players who are praying usually aren't shown on television, and people in the stands often don't notice because they're too busy rushing for the exits. But the players appreciate the after-game prayers, says Howard Cross of the Giants, because they serve as a "reality check," an opportunity to calm down and thank God for safety in the game.[4]

When a writer for *Sports Illustrated* objected to the practice, several officials in the NFL tried to stop the players from praying, saying that the gatherings at midfield violated the 1981 anti-fraternization rule—a rule usually applied to prevent players from dating NFL cheerleaders. (I'm not sure how they came up with that logic!) The officials threatened to impose $25,000 fines on team owners if their players continued to meet at midfield and pray.

In 1997, while we were preparing to go to New Orleans for the Super Bowl, people began to whisper that the league didn't want Reggie White leading the other players in prayer after the big game. According to *Miami Herald* sportswriter Armando Salguero, "Reggie said the NFL couldn't dictate to him what he did after a game or who he prayed with."[5]

Sure enough, after the game, Reggie strolled out to midfield and knelt to pray, and the matter became a moot point. Because Reggie was so popular, I suppose they didn't want to make an example out of him. The league officially decided that as long as group prayers didn't interfere with postgame team or media obligations, the practice was more a reflection of sportsmanship and community than a distraction.[6]

I was really pleased with the way things turned out, and I thought the Christian players were doing a good job of maintaining a strong testimony for Christ in the NFL.

A few months ago, while I was listening to a Christian radio station, the host was talking about football players and in a roundabout way insinuated that they were not Christians.

I couldn't believe what I was hearing. Other people called in and agreed, so I dialed the station myself. When I got on the line—I think I was the last call to make it through before the show ended—I introduced myself and said that the NFL is not bad, and it can provide a platform for good works. Professional football players have done a lot for people in need. But you rarely hear about the good things. People are always more eager to hear about the bad.

I would never call myself a minister, but I know I've been able to do things for people because of the visibility I have as Brett Favre's wife. I read the Bible, I know what it takes to be a Christian, and I try my best to glorify God through my testimony, and to let people see the faith aspect of my life.

It's not always easy. A lot of people who consider themselves evangelical Christians don't understand much about the Catholic Church. I'll admit that I don't know the history and background of a lot of other religions, but I do know that the characteristic that marks a true Christian, no matter what church he or she attends, is belief in Jesus Christ. And *belief* is one of those words with shades of meaning.

Many people believe that Jesus existed, that he literally walked the earth as the Son of God. Others agree with his teachings about loving their fellow man and doing good for others, but that's as far as their "belief" goes. Their opinions about Jesus Christ don't really affect their daily lives. But there's another way to believe, and this is the kind of belief that marks a true Christian. We need to believe that Jesus was sent to be our Savior and that he died for us. And we need to believe in Jesus enough to be confident that we can go to him with our deepest fears and problems.

A child's faith

I remember going to two weeks of Bible school every summer when I was young. We called it catechism, and that's where we learned a lot about God. In the fourth grade, my girl-friends and I would get into little cat fights, and I remember sitting through one of those Bible school days and thinking about my bad behavior—I knew God was disappointed in me. I knew he was speaking to me, because I felt so bad.

Another time, we had a week of revival, where we went to church every night. I was probably in third or fourth grade, and I remember feeling really convicted about a spat I'd had with a friend at school. I apologized to her the next day. Afterward, I felt warmth and forgiveness flood my heart as the weight of guilt lifted off my shoulders. I knew it was the right thing to do. I knew I was forgiven and all was well.

I first learned about God—and how to get along with others—in my family and in a tiny white church known as Infant of Prague. I have a picture of my mom and me stand-ing outside that church on the day of my First Communion. Later, the parish built a new church building not far away and renamed it St. Matthew's.

As a mother, I want my girls to be the best they can be in every aspect of their lives. I pray all the time that they will become women of faith, because everything else in life falls into place with that priority in order. I pray that they will come to a genuine faith early in life. Though I feel as if I have believed in Christ my entire life, I would have made better decisions and choices as a young person had I known more about what it really means to follow him. I didn't change my habits until after I made some bad decisions.

I always pray that my girls will be protected and that God will send an angel with them wherever they go. I want them to be successful on their own and not feel as if they're under a cloud of expectation to do something great because of their dad. I want them to be happy with what God leads them to do and be.

As I write this, Brittany is getting ready to start college. I've told her that while she lived at home, she was responsible to me and Brett for the choices she made. When she leaves home, the choices she makes will be between her and God. Now her responsibility will be much greater.

When you are a Christian

Some people think that Christians are holier-than-thou, self-righteous snobs who look down on everyone else. That's not at all true of the Christians I have met in the NFL and else-where. Genuine Christians know they have faults; they know they're far from perfect.

They're not trusting in their own goodness. They're trusting in the holy perfection of Jesus Christ.

Not long ago, someone sent me a poem. I was delighted when the author, Carol Wimmer, gave me permission to share it with you:

> When I say, "I am a Christian,"
> I'm not shouting, "I've been saved!"
> I'm whispering, "I get lost!
> That's why I chose this way."

When I say, "I am a Christian,"
I don't speak with human pride,
I'm confessing that I stumble—
needing God to be my guide.

When I say, "I am a Christian,"
I'm not trying to be strong,
I'm professing that I'm weak
and pray for strength to carry on.

When I say, "I am a Christian,"
I'm not bragging of success,
I'm admitting that I've failed
and cannot ever pay the debt.

When I say, "I am a Christian,"
I don't think I know it all,
I submit to my confusion,
asking humbly to be taught.

When I say, "I am a Christian,"
I'm not claiming to be perfect.
My flaws are far too visible,
but God believes I'm worth it.

When I say, "I am a Christian,"
I still feel the sting of pain,
I have my share of heartache,
which is why I seek His name.

When I say, "I am a Christian,"
I do not wish to judge.
I have no authority—
I only know I'm loved.[7]

I love Carol's poem because it expresses such an important truth: we're not perfect. I'm not perfect by any means, and I'm not trying to put myself forward as some great role model. I'm only trying to be an encouragement and an example, maybe even an inspiration, for women going through breast cancer. Bad things have happened to me. I've made poor choices. I'm not perfect, and I want people to know that.

Bad things have happened to me. I've made poor choices. I'm not perfect, and I want people to know that.

For some reason, God likes to use people who aren't perfect. I want to be available for him to use me. I want people to be able to learn from my mistakes, but not hold me up as a role model. I've learned a lot of hard lessons in my life, and I've learned a lot from my mistakes. I'm a better person because of that, a better Christian, and I believe I will end up with God someday. I'm excited about that coming day, even though I know there are a lot of things I'll have to answer for.

We all need to realize that we don't ultimately answer to one another, so we don't need to judge other people. We have to answer to just one person in the end—Jesus Christ. I'm trying to keep that in mind each day.

Quiet spirituality

Some people are naturally quiet and shy. And I've learned it's okay to be a quiet Christian. My mother is a spiritual person, but she's not very outspoken about her relationship with God. Yet as I was growing up, I remember seeing her sit by her bed and read her Bible every night. She wore the cover off that Bible, she handled it so much.

Christie and I found that old Bible a few years ago, and

we brought it out and looked at it, grateful for our memories of that book in our mother's hands. Mom taught us to go to church and respect Sunday and nourish our relationship with the Lord, but hers was a quiet example.

Besides being naturally shy, I was raised in and still attend a Catholic church, so I am not accustomed to some practices that are common for some of my other Christian friends. For instance, I'm uncomfortable praying aloud. If I'm asked to pray aloud in a meeting, I end up being so worried about all the ways I could get it wrong that I'm no longer thinking about God.

Once, I was involved in a Bible study that met in a private home. The leader opened by saying that at some point during the year, he would ask each of us to lead the others in prayer. I pulled him aside after that first study and told him that I was too shy to pray aloud. "Don't worry about it," he told me. "Because I *am* going to call on you and you'll be fine."

I can't tell you how much that bothered me. His "promise," which felt more like a threat, hung over my head like a thundercloud, blocking all the joy I should have been receiving from the time of study and fellowship. From the moment I sat down until it was time to leave, I worried about whether that would be the night I'd be called on to pray. I do pray—I pray all the time in my heart and mind—but I'm simply too reserved to unveil my heart in public, and on the spot.

One night at the study, we discussed a chapter called "Worthy or Unworthy?" in a book we were reading together. I read a verse and was asked what it meant, and I accidentally said, "I am worthy." I should have said, "We are loved."

I intended to continue and say that even though we had done nothing to deserve Christ's love, apparently he saw us as people worth redeeming. But I never got a chance to finish my thought. The leader rushed on to the next person, leaving my partial answer hanging in mid-air.

I felt terrible. I wanted to snatch the words and stuff them back into my mouth. Did everyone in the room think I was some kind of egotist? Did they think I actually considered myself worthy of Christ's sacrifice?

It may sound silly, but I actually lost sleep over that incident. I can't believe I kept going to the study.

When the holidays rolled around, Brett and I hosted a party for our Bible study group. After a great dinner, the leader called the group into the den to offer a few concluding thoughts about the program. I was feeling pretty relaxed—the house looked lovely and festive, everyone was having a good time, and I'd made it through the entire course without being called on to pray aloud.

Then the leader's gaze fell on me. "Deanna," he said, his voice booming through the room. "Why don't you open us with prayer?"

I shook my head and firmly mouthed the word *no*.

"Yes," he said, just as firmly.

Breleigh, who was not much more than a baby, chose that moment to start crying, which rattled me even more. I needed to tend to her, but I couldn't just run out of the room. I had to say something.

"Dear Lord," I prayed, my words tumbling over each other as they piled out of my mouth, "please watch over our guys as they travel this weekend, and bless us."

Horrified and humiliated, I passed the prayer to Doug Pederson and rushed off to take care of Breleigh. The back of my neck burned as I fled the room, and I just knew that everyone in the room was looking at me and feeling sorry for me. The focus of everyone's attention had shifted to me. That's not what I wanted. That's not what prayer is supposed to be about.

Not all Christians are bold, and I don't think we all have to be. I think you can be a spiritual person and share your heart and your story and do it without standing on a corner and yelling at everyone who walks by.

No matter what our personal makeup, being a Christian means that every day we have to walk the walk and seek an intimate relationship with the Lord. That holy relationship is just like a marriage—we have to keep the relationship strong through communication and spending time together. You don't necessarily keep a relationship strong by being bold. You do it by being consistent, whatever your personality style might be.

You can be a spiritual person and share your heart and your story and do it without standing on a corner and yelling at everyone who walks by.

Don't bet against God

People often use sports terms as metaphors for life. Because Brett and I grew up playing sports, it's natural for us to think of life in terms of an athletic event. We view ourselves as trained athletes, we see our tragedies and challenges as part of the opposing team, and we envision God as the coach who's calling the plays. Even when he sends us out to face tough odds, we know we can trust his wisdom.

Sometimes we overcome the odds and score a victory. Sometimes we get knocked flat. But our coach is always there, ready to pick us up, show us what we did wrong, and teach us how to do better.

I have a real competitive streak—and Brett obviously does too. In high school, we both worked hard in practice, and the work was fun for us. I used to be excited about going to practice, and I knew my game schedule forward and backward. I wanted to be the best and win as many games as possible. If someone told me, "You can't run a mile in eight minutes," I'd say, "Oh, yes I can . . . and I will. Watch me."

Brett loves the challenge of the game, and the word *defeat* is not in his vocabulary. We both believe that athletes should go out and do the best they can, giving it all they've got. We also believe that's all anyone can do.

When I played basketball, I remember telling myself, *The girl I'm guarding is not going to get any points.* When I visualized and verbalized my objective, it no longer mattered that the other girl might be taller and stronger.

Likewise, Brett doesn't have the best throwing mechanics in the NFL, but he has a champion's mentality. He's never been the most talented or the strongest player on the field, but he's always the most determined.

I've watched him fall, get up, and dust himself off many times. I'm amazed at how he always comes back stronger and better than ever. No matter what the adversity, he always comes out on top. I've watched him play football through so many injuries—and I know how bad they are because I see him at home—yet he always manages to smile and claim the victory. He has the best mentality and attitude when it comes to a challenge.

Brett truly is a role model for me. Every time something happens to me, I think about what he's been through and how he got through it with a good attitude. He's a class act, and he's done some pretty awesome things for a lot of people. He worked very hard to become the Brett Favre that everyone sees out on the field. It didn't just happen; he worked for his title as "the toughest man in football."

Sometimes I think we should measure success not by what a person accomplishes, but by the amount of adversity he or she overcomes. The simple act of standing is a lot harder for a person who's just had a knee replacement than it is for a healthy teenager.

If you want to beat cancer or grief or a lack of education or whatever's standing in your way, you need to develop this kind of determination. How do you do it? It's simply a matter of making the right choices.

When I was struggling with chemo, I

I think we should measure success not by what a person accomplishes, but by the amount of adversity he or she overcomes.

realized that if I chose to be a victim, that's all I would ever be. Every day I'd lie in bed and look at the ceiling and tell myself, *I can stay in bed and mope about how bad I feel—and be a moper. Or I can get out of bed, get dressed, and try to accomplish something on my to-do list. It might take me all day, but at least I'll be an achiever.*

If I made it my goal to overcome something, and set my mind to it, I knew I could do it.

We are all given the same twenty-four hours every day, and we all have special abilities. Something unique exists in each of us, so we need to find the motivation and strength to express our specific gifts. You may be an executive, a teacher, a dancer, or an athlete. You may be an organizer, a hostess, or a nurturer. Whatever your gift, whatever your odds, you can find a way to overcome adversity.

You can either give up when life gets tough, or you can say, "I'm not going to be defeated. I'm going to listen to the experts, I'm going to do what I have to do, and I'm going to get through this."

I hope I've given you enough examples so that you know I had my share of low moments during the course of my cancer treatment. There were times when I'd catch a glimpse of myself in the mirror and think, *Wow—am I sick? Are people looking at me like I'm sick?*

But if you dwell on those moments, you'll begin to feel sorry for yourself—and it's hard to stop a pity party once it's in full swing. I used to have them, believe me. I'd start crying and find that I couldn't stop the tears. But eventually I'd pick myself up, brush myself off, and resolve to get through the next hour as a *victor,* not a victim. You have to *choose* to move forward.

I never felt it was my place to ask God why I got cancer. I didn't want to blame or question him, yet I often found myself wondering what God planned to do with my experience.

Some of those answers were revealed when I began to get letters from women who had gone through situations far worse than mine. My story was touching women who had been diagnosed at stage IV, or who'd undergone mastectomies. That knowledge was comforting, but even more affirming were the letters I got from doctors and other health professionals who said that women were coming in to be checked "because of Deanna Favre." When I learned that these check-ups had resulted in a couple of early detections, I began to understand how God was using my cancer for good.

I know there are no guarantees in this life. I know that cancer can recur, and frankly, I'll be devastated if mine does. When I meet women who are going through chemo for the second or third time, my heart always skips a beat.

For the first year after my cancer treatments ended, I had to go to the oncologist every three months for an exam. For the second year, I went every six months for a follow-up mammogram and ultrasound. In this third year, I'm going to the doctor every six months for either a mammogram or an MRI.

I'll be honest. Every time I go in, I hold my breath until I hear someone say, "You're clear—everything looks good." If they're a little slow coming out with the results, I always start to wonder, *Did they find something?*

What if my cancer recurs? To be honest, I'll grieve for a while. And then I'll pick myself up and try to remain positive. I'll focus on following my doctors' advice and being well.

And I'll keep praying.

Because God brought me through cancer the first time and used it for good, I know he could do it again. And someday, when he chooses to take me home, I pray that my passing out of this life will glorify him even more than my remaining in it.

If you have been diagnosed with breast cancer

If you have been diagnosed with breast cancer, you should know that you are a member of a powerful sorority. Know you're not alone. Thousands of women have walked this path before you, and we want you to learn from our experience.

I urge you to learn all you can and hold tight to your hope. Don't give in. Don't accept the role of victim. Be positive. Be willing to put up a fight and defeat the cancer. Stay as healthy as possible. Try to maintain as normal a life as possible and be a positive example for others. You never know who is watching, and someone close to you—your sister, your daughter, your friend—may later be diagnosed with this same disease. They may learn a lot from you and draw strength from you.

Remain a fighter, and don't let cancer take over. Stay positive and stay in the fight.

Faith is extremely important. I can't imagine getting through some of the things I've experienced without it. It's easy to wait until something bad happens and only then think, *Maybe God can help me with this.*

But God is always there. He's like a proud parent when good things are happening for us, and he's a comforting parent when bad things come along. Realizing that you can find comfort in faith is a huge part of getting through tragedy or cancer or whatever you might be going through.

Jesus said, "I tell you the truth, if you had faith even as small as a mustard seed, you could say to this mountain, 'Move from here to there,' and it would move. Nothing would be impossible."[8]

Through Christ, we can do anything within God's will. We can trust that we're going to come out on the other side and everything's going to be okay. This realization gives us a strength that we're not capable of on our own. It's huge. I may not know exactly how big or powerful God is, but I know my faith has given me an amazing strength to endure all kinds of things.

The entire first year after my chemo, every time a breast cancer patient came up to me, there were always tears in my eyes and in hers. A kindred spirit exists between those of us who have walked the path of breast cancer. You know that these other women know what you've been through, and vice versa. Right after being introduced, we feel an overwhelming sensation, knowing we have shared experiences.

After I told my story at an event for a breast cancer walk, a lady came up to me and said, "You saved my life."

Wow. I looked at her, dumbfounded, as she said, "I had a lump in my breast. Because of you, when your story came out, I decided I'd better go get the lump checked out. It was malignant; so you saved my life."

At the time we met, this lady didn't have her hair because she was going through chemo. I hugged her and felt used by God. Obviously, he wanted my story to come out.

Years ago, I was such a private person that I'd have said,

"I'm just going to keep this to myself." Now that I think about it, I must have been frequently in contact with women who were going through breast cancer treatment. They were suffering and enduring in silence.

Since that first encounter, I've had many women come up and tell me that they're going through breast cancer. I love hearing about how I might have touched them. I truly believe that those women help me more than I help them, because they encourage me to continue sharing my story and trying to touch other lives. This is awesome for me. I really believe it's all the work of God's hand. I can't take any credit for it, but I'm so happy to be used.

I love the title of this book. It comes from a statement Brett made during a press conference after he finished his drug rehab. When a reporter asked him if he was worried about suffering a relapse, Brett said, "All I can tell people is, 'If you don't believe me, bet against me,' because eventually they'll lose." One reason the title resonates with me is that I've been inspired by Brett's positive attitude. Watching him go through drug addiction and seeing him come out on the other side has given me courage. A lot of people don't understand that addiction is a disease that takes hold of your life and affects everything.

It takes a positive attitude to beat cancer and to recover from other tragedies in life.

In professional football, the Super Bowl is the big prize, and it takes a lot to get there. But even fresh out of rehab, Brett was confident that he could overcome his addiction and win the Super Bowl. In the same way, it takes a positive attitude to beat cancer and to recover from other tragedies in life.

When adversity strikes, people sometimes lose faith in

themselves, in people around them, and in God. They wonder, *Why did this have to happen to me?*

But with a great attitude, a winning spirit, and faith, no adversity or tragedy is insurmountable. "Don't bet against me!" is my way of saying that I know I have all the tools I need to win the battle, because I know what it takes to overcome. I know in my heart that God won't let me down.

I know I'm going to win, so don't bet against me.

And don't let anyone bet against you.

A letter from Breleigh Favre
to kids whose moms are fighting breast cancer:

I love my mom. Sometimes she does silly things like dancing in front of company when there isn't any music on, but that's okay.

I'm a dancer too, and when I'm dancing and I look out in the audience and see my mom smiling at me, it makes me feel so good! And when I'm done, she always gives me a hug and says, "I'm so proud of you!"

Well, I'm proud of her too!

When she got sick, it was really scary. The worst part was when her hair fell out, because I love playing with her hair. But to help her feel better, my dad shaved his hair off and my sister, Brittany, and I cut our hair real short, too.

Everybody's hair has grown back now—except my dad's. He still cuts his real short!

If your mom is sick, you can help her a lot by just doing things for her. You can sit and read with her, talk with her, and if she asks you to do something—just do it, even if you don't want to. Most important, tell her that you love her and that you're proud of her.

I was scared when my mom got sick, but she was really strong and she got through it.

I hope your mom gets better, too!

In the world of teenage daughters, we tend to push our parents as far away from our lives as possible.

Despite our love and appreciation for them, the relationship quickly turns into one we would like to keep within the privacy of our own home as best we can. Our once carefree thoughts become fixated on the constant humiliation brought to us by their outlandish behavior, dress, or appearance. We assume parents are here only to pay for things and embarrass us in front of our friends.

I have been told numerous times of my mother's beauty, both spiritual and physical, but my own selfishness hid that beauty from me. But if anything can tear down the walls of separation between mother and daughter, it would be the fear of losing her.

My mother's battle with cancer not only revealed her strength to the world—it revealed her strength to me, as well. Sadly, I lived with her for sixteen years before I really knew her. With the threat of losing her hanging over my head, I realized that she wasn't out to ruin my life; she was actually trying to make it as enjoyable as possible. Her efforts for family time weren't meant to destroy my social life; they were efforts to make my life more fulfilling.

I am almost envious of my little sister, Breleigh, because her heart of gold holds such an innocent and pure love for our mother, attainable only by complete selflessness. That is the type of love our mom has instilled in Bre, and the same type of love I have received my entire life.

Her work speaks for itself. She has used her battle to empower women all over the country who are fighting the same disease. Instead of taking her struggle lying down, she fought her fight and is using that power to help others.

Through her struggle, I have discovered the most beautiful woman I have ever met. Even though as my mother she is still cheesy at times and sometimes a little embarrassing, she is an inspiration to me. I will always strive to attain her compassion and purity, and to live by her example.

a basic breast cancer vocabulary

Aromatase: an enzyme that helps produce estrogen. Aromatase is found in the adrenal glands, the ovaries, the brain, and adipose (fat) tissues.

Aromatase inhibitors: drugs usually given to cancer patients to lower the amount of estrogen in the body.

Aspirate: to withdraw fluid or cells from a lump, cyst, or suspected tumor.

Biopsy: a procedure that removes a tissue sample, which can then be examined under a microscope as the doctor searches for cancer cells.

Chemotherapy: the treatment of cancer by using drugs that kill rapidly dividing cells.

Complete mastectomy (includes simple, modified radical, and radical): removal of the entire breast that contains cancer.

Cyst: a sac or cavity in the body containing fluid.

Ductal carcinoma in situ (DCIS): the condition of abnormal cells found in the lining of a breast duct. It is a non-invasive malignant tumor also called intraductal carcinoma. Because it *can* progress and become invasive, a woman should consult with her doctor about possible treatment.

Early stage breast cancer: invasive breast cancers are categorized as stage I, II, III, or IV. Stages I and II are considered "early stage" and usually refer to small tumors that have not spread.

Endometriosis: a condition in which tissue that usually lines the uterus and is shed each month grows *outside* the uterus. Endometriosis can result in painful cramps and infertility.

Estrogen: a hormone that promotes the growth of female characteristics in the body.

Estrogen receptor: a special type of protein found on some cancer cells. When estrogen attaches to it, it can cause the cancer to grow.

Estrogen receptor negative: breast cancer cells without estrogen receptors (also known as ER-).

Estrogen receptor positive: breast cancer cells with estrogen receptors. These cells depend on estrogen to grow (also known as ER+).

Fibroadenoma: a benign (non-cancerous) tumor, usually found in the breast, of mixed fibrous and glandular tissue.

Fibrocystic breast disease: noncancerous cysts in the breast.

Hormone receptor: a protein within or on the outside of a cell. If attached to a certain hormone, the receptor will cause changes within the cell.

Invasive: a malignant tumor that grows into surrounding tissues. Invasive tumors are more likely to spread to other parts of the body.

Lobular: each breast is made up of up to twenty sections called "lobes." Each lobe is made up of smaller "lobules" where milk is made. Lobes and lobules are connected by ducts, or small tubes, that carry milk to the nipple.

Lobular carcinoma in situ (LCIS): a benign condition that consists of abnormal cells in the lining of a lobule. LCIS is not cancer, but it means a woman has an increased risk of developing breast cancer.

Lumpectomy: surgical removal of the tumor only.

Lymph nodes: swellings of the lymphatic system found throughout the body. They filter lymphatic fluid, essential for a functioning immune system, and store lymphocytes, a type of white blood cell.

Lymphedema: swelling of the arm, a side effect experienced by less than 20 percent of patients after lymph node removal. Early signs of lymphedema are a feeling of tightness in the arm, pain or aching in the arm, swelling of the arm, and loss of movement or flexibility in the arm. One of the first signs patients notice is that rings or sleeves no longer fit.

Mammogram: an X-ray of the soft tissue of the breast.

Mammotome: Brand name of a device made by Johnson & Johnson Ethicon Endo-Surgery that uses a computer-guided probe to perform a vacuum-assisted breast biopsy.

Margin: the area of normal breast tissue immediately around a malignant tumor. When a tumor is removed in a lumpectomy, the surgeon will examine the margins to see if the area is cancer-free. If so, the cancer has probably not spread beyond the initial tumor.

Metastasize: to spread to other parts of the body.

MIBB (Minimally Invasive Breast Biopsy): Brand name of a device made by Tyco/United States Surgical Corporation that uses a computer-guided probe to perform a vacuum-assisted breast biopsy.

Neutropenia: a common side effect of chemotherapy that occurs when too many white blood cells are destroyed and the patient's immune system is weakened so it cannot fight infection. Neutropenia can lead to other complications and delay proper treatment.

Oncology: the study and treatment of cancer.

Oncologist: one who studies and treats cancer.

Onychomadesis: the separation of a fingernail or toenail from the nail bed. Often a side effect of cancer treatments.

Partial mastectomy: removal of the part of the breast that contains cancer.

Peripherally inserted central catheter (PICC) line: a special IV line used to insert fluids into a vein.

Port: a surgically implanted device through which blood can be drawn and drugs administered without repeated needle sticks.

Private patient: a patient insured by private medical insurance.

Public patient: a patient whose medical bills will be at least partially covered by Medicare.

Radiation: the process of using X-ray radiation to kill cancer cells. The advantage of radiation is that it is focused on small areas, limiting the danger to healthy cells.

For a much more complete (and fun!) dictionary, visit www. breastcancer.org/dictionary/ and hear your favorite entertainment celebrities pronounce and define breast cancer terms.

what to read when . . .

Angela Hunt and I have pulled together some of our favorite verses to read during tough times. We hope they will inspire and comfort you, as well.

A friend is discouraged

Wise words are like deep waters; wisdom flows from the wise like a bubbling brook.   PROVERBS 18:4

The human spirit can endure a sick body, but who can bear a crushed spirit?   PROVERBS 18:14

You are worried

Give your burdens to the LORD, and he will take care of you.
He will not permit the godly to slip and fall.   PSALM 55:22

Don't worry about anything; instead, pray about everything. Tell God what you need, and thank him for all he has done. Then you will experience God's peace, which exceeds anything we can understand. His peace will guard your hearts and minds as you live in Christ Jesus. PHILIPPIANS 4:6-7

Give all your worries and cares to God, for he cares about you. I PETER 5:7

You are suffering

Yet what we suffer now is nothing compared to the glory he will reveal to us later. . . . For we know that all creation has been groaning as in the pains of childbirth right up to the present time. And we believers also groan, even though we have the Holy Spirit within us as a foretaste of future glory, for we long for our bodies to be released from sin and suffering. We, too, wait with eager hope for the day when God will give us our full rights as his adopted children, including the new bodies he has promised us. ROMANS 8:18, 22-23

That is why we never give up. Though our bodies are dying, our spirits are being renewed every day. For our present troubles are small and won't last very long. Yet they produce for us a glory that vastly outweighs them and will last forever! So we don't look at the troubles we can see now; rather, we fix our gaze on things that cannot be seen. For the things we see now will soon be gone, but the things we cannot see will last forever. 2 CORINTHIANS 4:16-18

In everything we do, we show that we are true ministers of God. We patiently endure troubles and hardships and calamities of every kind. We have been beaten, been put in prison, faced angry mobs, worked to exhaustion, endured sleepless nights, and gone without food. We prove ourselves by our purity, our understanding, our patience, our kindness, by the Holy Spirit within us, and by our sincere love. We faithfully preach the truth. God's power is working in us. We use the weapons of righteousness in the right hand for attack and the left hand for defense. We serve God whether people honor us or despise us, whether they slander us or praise us. We are honest, but they call us imposters. We are ignored, even though we are well known. We live close to death, but we are still alive. We have been beaten, but we have not been killed. Our hearts ache, but we always have joy. We are poor, but we give spiritual riches to others. We own nothing, and yet we have everything. 2 CORINTHIANS 6:4-10

You wonder why

"My thoughts are nothing like your thoughts," says the LORD. "And my ways are far beyond anything you could imagine. For just as the heavens are higher than the earth, so my ways are higher than your ways and my thoughts higher than your thoughts." ISAIAH 55:8-9

Dear brothers and sisters, when troubles come your way, consider it an opportunity for great joy. For you know that when your faith is tested, your endurance has a chance to grow. So let it grow, for when your endurance is fully developed, you will be perfect and complete, needing nothing. JAMES 1:2-4

God blesses those who patiently endure testing and temptation. Afterward they will receive the crown of life that God has promised to those who love him. JAMES 1:12

So be truly glad. There is wonderful joy ahead, even though you have to endure many trials for a little while. These trials will show that your faith is genuine. It is being tested as fire tests and purifies gold—though your faith is far more precious than mere gold. So when your faith remains strong through many trials, it will bring you much praise and glory and honor on the day when Jesus Christ is revealed to the whole world.   I PETER 1:6-7

You are sick

> Oh, the joys of those who are kind to the poor!
>> The LORD rescues them when they are in trouble.
> The LORD protects them
>> and keeps them alive.
> He gives them prosperity in the land
>> and rescues them from their enemies.
> The LORD nurses them when they are sick
>> and restores them to health.   PSALM 41:1-3

Are any of you sick? You should call for the elders of the church to come and pray over you, anointing you with oil in the name of the Lord. Such a prayer offered in faith will heal the sick, and the Lord will make you well. And if you have committed any sins, you will be forgiven.   JAMES 5:14-15

You feel as if God has abandoned you

> I look up to the mountains—
>> does my help come from there?
> My help comes from the LORD,
>> who made heaven and earth!

He will not let you stumble;
the one who watches over you will not slumber.
Indeed, he who watches over Israel
never slumbers or sleeps.

The LORD himself watches over you!
The LORD stands beside you as your protective shade.
The sun will not harm you by day,
nor the moon at night.

The LORD keeps you from all harm
and watches over your life.
The LORD keeps watch over you as you come and go,
both now and forever.   PSALM 121

Your prayers seem ineffective

[Jesus prayed,] "Father, if you are willing, please take this cup of suffering away from me. Yet I want your will to be done, not mine."   LUKE 22:42

So to keep me from becoming proud, I was given a thorn in my flesh, a messenger from Satan to torment me and keep me from becoming proud. Three different times I begged the Lord to take it away. Each time he said, "My grace is all you need. My power works best in weakness." So now I am glad to boast about my weaknesses, so that the power of Christ can work through me. That's why I take pleasure in my weaknesses, and in the insults, hardships, persecutions, and troubles that I suffer for Christ. For when I am weak, then I am strong.   2 CORINTHIANS 12:7-10

You are discouraged

> *Then call on me when you are in trouble,*
> *and I will rescue you,*
> *and you will give me glory.* PSALM 50:15

> *Let all that I am praise the LORD;*
> *with my whole heart, I will praise his holy name.*
> *Let all that I am praise the LORD;*
> *may I never forget the good things he does for me.*
> *He forgives all my sins*
> *and heals all my diseases.*
> *He redeems me from death*
> *and crowns me with love and tender mercies.*
> *He fills my life with good things.*
> *My youth is renewed like the eagle's!* PSALM 103:1-5

You are depressed

> *The LORD is close to the brokenhearted; he rescues those whose*
> *spirits are crushed.* PSALM 34:18

> *For the despondent, every day brings trouble;*
> *for the happy heart, life is a continual feast.* PROVERBS 15:15

> *A cheerful heart is good medicine,*
> *but a broken spirit saps a person's strength.* PROVERBS 17:22

You feel mixed up and confused

Look, God is greater than we can understand. His years cannot be counted. JOB 36:26

> *For everything there is a season,*
> *a time for every activity under heaven.*

A time to be born and a time to die.
A time to plant and a time to harvest.
A time to kill and a time to heal.
A time to tear down and a time to build up.
A time to cry and a time to laugh.
A time to grieve and a time to dance.
A time to scatter stones and a time to gather stones.
A time to embrace and a time to turn away.
A time to search and a time to quit searching.
A time to keep and a time to throw away.
A time to tear and a time to mend.
A time to be quiet and a time to speak.
A time to love and a time to hate.
A time for war and a time for peace.   ECCLESIASTES 3:1-8

You need strength

God is our refuge and strength,
always ready to help in times of trouble.
So we will not fear when earthquakes come
and the mountains crumble into the sea.
Let the oceans roar and foam.
Let the mountains tremble as the waters surge! . . .
"Be still, and know that I am God!
I will be honored by every nation.
I will be honored throughout the world."   PSALM 46:1-3, 10

Have you never heard?
Have you never understood?
The LORD is the everlasting God,
the Creator of all the earth.
He never grows weak or weary.
No one can measure the depths of his understanding.

He gives power to the weak
    and strength to the powerless.
Even youths will become weak and tired,
    and young men will fall in exhaustion.
But those who trust in the LORD will find new strength.
    They will soar high on wings like eagles.
They will run and not grow weary.
    They will walk and not faint.   ISAIAH 40:28-31

Don't be afraid, for I am with you.
    Don't be discouraged, for I am your God.
I will strengthen you and help you.
    I will hold you up with my victorious right hand.

                                        ISAIAH 41:10

I can do everything through Christ, who gives me strength.

                                        PHILIPPIANS 4:13

You are afraid

"This is my command—be strong and courageous! Do not be afraid or discouraged. For the LORD your God is with you wherever you go."   JOSHUA 1:9

But when I am afraid,
    I will put my trust in you.
I praise God for what he has promised.
    I trust in God, so why should I be afraid?
    What can mere mortals do to me?   PSALM 56:3-4

And this same God who takes care of me will supply all your needs from his glorious riches, which have been given to us in Christ Jesus.   PHILIPPIANS 4:19

You want to do something to help others

The earth is the LORD's, and everything in it.
The world and all its people belong to him.   PSALM 24:1

No, this is the kind of fasting I want:
Free those who are wrongly imprisoned;
*   lighten the burden of those who work for you.*
Let the oppressed go free,
*   and remove the chains that bind people.*
Share your food with the hungry,
*   and give shelter to the homeless.*
Give clothes to those who need them,
*   and do not hide from relatives who need your help.*

Then your salvation will come like the dawn,
*   and your wounds will quickly heal.*
Your godliness will lead you forward,
*   and the glory of the LORD will protect you from behind.*
Then when you call, the LORD will answer.
*   "Yes, I am here," he will quickly reply.*   ISAIAH 58:6-9

Then [Jesus] turned to his host. "When you put on a luncheon or a banquet," he said, "don't invite your friends, brothers, relatives, and rich neighbors. For they will invite you back, and that will be your only reward. Instead, invite the poor, the crippled, the lame, and the blind. Then at the resurrection of the righteous, God will reward you for inviting those who could not repay you."   LUKE 14:12-14

Remember this—a farmer who plants only a few seeds will get a small crop. But the one who plants generously will get a generous crop. You must each decide in your heart how much to give. And don't give reluctantly or in response to pressure.

"For God loves a person who gives cheerfully." And God will generously provide all you need. Then you will always have everything you need and plenty left over to share with others. 2 CORINTHIANS 9:6-8

You need hope

> *Why am I discouraged? Why is my heart so sad? I will put*
> *my hope in God! I will praise him again—my Savior and*
> *my God!* PSALM 42:11

> *"For I know the plans I have for you," says the LORD. "They*
> *are plans for good and not for disaster, to give you a future*
> *and a hope."* JEREMIAH 29:11

You are thankful

> *I will praise you, LORD, with all my heart;*
> *I will tell of all the marvelous things you have done.*
> *I will be filled with joy because of you.*
> *I will sing praises to your name, O Most High.*
> PSALM 9:1-2

> *It is good to give thanks to the LORD,*
> *to sing praises to the Most High.*
> *It is good to proclaim your unfailing love in the morning,*
> *your faithfulness in the evening,*
> *accompanied by the ten-stringed harp*
> *and the melody of the lyre.*

> *You thrill me, LORD, with all you have done for me!*
> *I sing for joy because of what you have done.*
> *O LORD, what great works you do!*
> *And how deep are your thoughts.* PSALM 92:1-5

You are too overwhelmed to pray

> I love the LORD because he hears my voice
>   and my prayer for mercy.
> Because he bends down to listen,
>   I will pray as long as I have breath!
> Death wrapped its ropes around me;
>   the terrors of the grave overtook me.
>   I saw only trouble and sorrow.
> Then I called on the name of the LORD:
>   "Please, LORD, save me!"
> How kind the LORD is! How good he is!
>   So merciful, this God of ours!
> The Lord protects those of childlike faith;
>   I was facing death, and he saved me. PSALM 116:1-6

And the Holy Spirit helps us in our weakness. For example, we don't know what God wants us to pray for. But the Holy Spirit prays for us with groanings that cannot be expressed in words. And the Father who knows all hearts knows what the Spirit is saying, for the Spirit pleads for us believers in harmony with God's own will. And we know that God causes everything to work together for the good of those who love God and are called according to his purpose for them.

ROMANS 8:26-28

Someone has died

> The LORD cares deeply
>   when his loved ones die. PSALM 116:15

You want to know what true love is

Love is patient and kind. Love is not jealous or boastful or proud or rude. It does not demand its own way. It is not irritable, and it keeps no record of being wronged. It does not rejoice about injustice but rejoices whenever the truth wins out. Love never gives up, never loses faith, is always hopeful, and endures through every circumstance. . . .

When I was a child, I spoke and thought and reasoned as a child. But when I grew up, I put away childish things. Now we see things imperfectly as in a cloudy mirror, but then we will see everything with perfect clarity. All that I know now is partial and incomplete, but then I will know everything completely, just as God now knows me completely.

Three things will last forever—faith, hope, and love—and the greatest of these is love.   I CORINTHIANS 13:4-7, 11-13

Dear children, let's not merely say that we love each other; let us show the truth by our actions. Our actions will show that we belong to the truth, so we will be confident when we stand before God.   I JOHN 3:18-19 *for more information*

If you or someone you love has been diagnosed with cancer, the following information might prove helpful:

Deanna Favre HOPE Foundation
http://www.DeannaFavre4Hope.com
Donations and requests for assistance can be sent to the foundation's attention at 1 Willow Bend Dr., Hattiesburg, MS 39402. Please include your name, address, and telephone number with your donation or request.

National Cancer Institute
(800) 422-6237, http://cancer.gov/

Cancer Information Service
(800) 422-6237, http://cis.nci.nih.gov/

National Research Center for Women and Families
(202) 223-4000
http://www.center4research.org/womenhlth1.
html#BreastCancer

Don't bet against me!

National "Get A Mammogram: Do It for Yourself, Do It for Your Family" Campaign

(800) 422-6237
http://www.cancer.gov/cancerinfo/breasthealth
Brochures in English, Chinese, Filipino, and Vietnamese

National Breast Cancer Coalition

(800) 622-2838
http://www.natlbcc.org/

National Breast and Cervical Cancer Early Detection Program

(888) 842-6355
http://www.cdc.gov/cancer/nbccedp/index.htm

Susan G. Komen for the Cure

(972) 855-1600 (headquarters)
(800) I'M AWARE® (helpline)
http://cms.komen.org/komen/index.htm

CHAPTER 1: WORLD CHAMPIONS

1. "Timeline: Brett Favre," *Sports Illustrated Scrapbook,* http://sportsillustrated.cnn.com/football/nfl/features/favre/timeline.
2. "Sunday Conversation: Brett Favre," Special to ESPN.com, http://sports.espn.go.com/nfl/news/story?id=1930185.
3. Ibid.

CHAPTER 4: FUMBLE AND RECOVERY

1. Brett Favre with Chris Havel, *Favre: For the Record* (New York: Doubleday, 1997), 62–65.

CHAPTER 5: SUDDEN DEATH

1. Job 1:9-12.
2. Job 1:21.
3. Packers–Raiders Recap, http://www.packers.com/news/releases/2003/12/24/3/.
4. Ibid.

CHAPTER 6: BACK-TO-BACK LOSSES

1. 1 Corinthians 13:4-7.
2. "Enabling: A Form of Codependence," The Good Shepherd Restoration Ministries, http://www.tgsrm.org/Enabling.html.

CHAPTER 7: SUDDENLY SIDELINED

1. Job 2:3-7.
2. "Breast Biopsy," Oncology Channel, http://www.oncologychannel. com/breastcancer/breastbiopsy/needleeshtml.
3. Ibid.

CHAPTER 8: TOUGH CALLS

1. Larry Weisman, "Deanna Favre Gives Green Bay Another Reason to Cheer," *USA Today,* October 19, 2005, http://www. usatoday.com/sports/football/nfl/packers/2005-10-19-deanna-favre-cover_x.htm.
2. "Lumpectomy," *Imaginis, The Breast Cancer Resource,* http://www. imaginis.com/breasthealth/lumpectomy2.asp#how.
3. "Breast Cancer: Sentinel Node Biopsy," http://www.webmd. com/breast-cancer/guide/sentinel-node-biopsy.

CHAPTER 9: PLAYING WITH PAIN

1. "Managing Chemo Side Effects," breastcancer.org, http://www. breastcancer.org/tre_sys_chemo_sideeff.html.
2. "How Chemo Works," breastcancer.org, http://www.breastcancer. org/tre_sys_chemo_whatis.html.
3. PICC lines (peripherally inserted central catheters), http://www. cancerbackup.org.uk/Treatments/Chemotherapy/Linesports/ PICCline.
4. Nancy Etcoff, *Survival of the Prettiest* (New York: Anchor Books, 1999), 95.
5. Ibid., 120.
6. Ibid.
7. Ibid., 123.
8. "Chemotherapy and You: A Guide to Self-Help During Cancer Treatment," National Cancer Institute, http://www.cancer. gov/cancertopics/chemotherapy-and-you/page4.
9. Marc Silver, "Love Her Tender," *U.S. News and World Report,* October 3, 2004, http://www.usnews.com/usnews/health/ articles/041011/11husbands_print.htm.
10. "Nail Disease," *Wikipedia,* http://en.wikipedia.org/wiki/ Nail_disease.

11. "Chemotherapy and Your Nails," breastcancer.org, http://www.breastcancer.org/hsn_your_nails.html.

12. Jane Gross, "Chemotherapy Fog Is No Longer Ignored as Illusion," *New York Times,* April 29, 2007, http://www.nytimes.com/2007/04/29/health/29chemo.html.

13. Ibid.

14. Ibid.

15. Ibid.

CHAPTER 10: THE HUDDLE

1. Information for this section is drawn in part from the following websites:

   "Cancer Myths," National Breast Cancer Foundation, Inc., http://www.nationalbreastcancer.org/about=breast=cancer/breast=cancer=myths.

   "Myths About Breast Cancer," http://www.breastcancer.org/cmn_myt_idx.html.

   "The Most Common Myths about Breast Cancer," *Women's Health Care,* http://www.mjbovo.com/BreastCaMyths.htm.

   "Top 10 Breast Cancer Myths Debunked," http://www.bcaction.org/index.php?page=breast=cancer=myths=debunked.

2. Clifton Fadiman, ed., *The Little, Brown Book of Anecdotes* (Boston: Little, Brown, 1985), 517–518.

3. James 5:14-15.

4. For example, see Psalm 115:3, Psalm 138:8, Proverbs 19:21, Isaiah 45:13, Daniel 4:34-35, Luke 13:32, Acts 17:27, Romans 9:17, Ephesians 3:10, and Revelation 17:17.

5. 1 John 5:14-15.

6. Matthew 6:9-13.

7. Philip Yancey, *Prayer: Does It Make Any Difference?* (Grand Rapids, Mich.: Zondervan, 2006), 228.

8. Nancy E. Robbins, *God's Madcap: The Story of Amy Carmichael* (Fort Washington, Pa.: Christian Literature Crusade, 1974), 14.

9. Colossians 1:17.

10. See Matthew 6:26.

11. Matthew 10:30-31.

12. Psalm 139:1-18.

13. James 1:2-4.
14. James 4:2-3.
15. Luke 11:5-13.

CHAPTER 11: MORE THAN A GAME

1. Larry Weisman, "As Crowds Adore Him, Favre Yearns for Quiet," *USA Today,* August 11, 2005, http://www.usatoday.com/sports/football/nfl/packers/2005-08-11-favre-cover-story_x.htm.
2. Clifton Fadiman, ed., *The Little, Brown Book of Anecdotes,* (Boston: Little, Brown, 1985), 91.
3. Daniel 2:17-19.
4. Acts 20:35.
5. Matthew 6:19-21.
6. Randy Alcorn, *The Treasure Principle* (Sisters, Ore.: Multnomah, 2001), 18.
7. Luke 12:48, NASB.

CHAPTER 12: POSTGAME PRESS

1. Paul Lagass, "Cancer," *The Columbia Encyclopedia,* sixth edition (New York: Columbia University Press, 2000), electronic edition.
2. Carolyn M. Kaelin, M.D., and Francesca Coltrera, "Cancer and Staying Fit," *Newsweek,* March 26, 2007, 70.
3. "Key Facts about Women's Cancers," H-Cup Highlights, Agency for Healthcare Research and Quality, http://www.hcup-us.ahrq.gov/reports/Highlights_2006_Final.pdf.
4. "Congressional Budget Office Cost Estimate," CBO, http://www.cbo.gov/ftpdoc.cfm?index=2147&type+0&sequence=0.
5. "Deanna Favre," *Wikipedia,* http://en.wikipedia.org/wiki/Deanna_Favre.
6. Susan Ramsett, "Deanna Favre: The Story Behind the Pink Green Bay Packer Caps," http://www.wsaw.com/news/headlines/2061591.html.
7. Sara Boyd, "10K 'quite a challenge,' but Deanna Favre beats goal time," *Green Bay Press Gazette,* June 9, 2007, http://www.greenbaypressgazette.com/apps/pbcs.dll/article?AID=/20070609/GPG02/70609019/1978.
8. Romans 8:28.

CHAPTER 13: WINNER'S TROPHY

1. Claudia Wallis and Alice Park, "Living with Cancer," *Time,* April 9, 2007, 39.
2. Ibid., 39.
3. Ibid., 40.
4. "Health: What Breast-Cancer Survivors Can Expect," *Newsweek,* April 2, 2007, 10.
5. "Early Stage Breast Cancer: A Patient and Doctor Dialogue," National Women's Health Information Center, http://www. womenshealth.gov/faq/earlybc.htm, March 2002.
6. "Diet and Lifestyle and Survival from Breast Cancer," Fact Sheet #44, June 2002, Sprecher Institute for Comparative Cancer Research, http://envirocancer.cornell.edu/factsheet/diet/fs44.survival.cfm.
7. Larry Weisman, "Deanna Favre Gives Green Bay Another Reason to Cheer," *USA Today,* October 19, 2005, http://www. usatoday.com/sports/football/nfl/packers/2005-10-19-deanna-favre-cover_x.htm.
8. Ross E. Carter, Ph.D. and Charlene A. Carter, Ph.D., "Communication in Couples with Breast Cancer," *HealthLink,* January 28, 1999, http://healthlink.mcw.edu/article/917588037.html.
9. Marc Silver, "Love Her Tender," *U.S. News and World Report,* October 3, 2004, http://www.usnews.com/usnews/health/articles/041011/11husbands_print.htm.
10. Ibid.
11. Ibid.
12. Oswald Chambers, *My Utmost for His Highest* (New York: Dodd, Mead, 1935), 215.

CHAPTER 14: FAITH FOR THE FUTURE

1. Job 31:35-37.
2. Job 42:3-6.
3. Job 42:12-17.
4. Ken Walker, "Feel the Real Power," *Today's Christian,* November/December 1997, http://www.christianitytoday.com/tc/7r6/7r6015.html.
5. Ibid.
6. Joe Starkey, "Steelers, Pirates, Pitt Football Incorporate Christianity into Team Framework," *Pittsburgh Tribune-Review,* June

26, 2005, http://www.pittsburghlive.com/x/pittsburghtrib/s_ 347621.html.

7. Carolyn Wimmer, "When I Say, 'I Am a Christian,'" copyright 1988 by Carolyn Wimmer. Used by permission.

8. Matthew 17:20.

Deanna Favre, wife of Green Bay Packers quarterback Brett Favre, was inadvertently thrust into the national spotlight when, in the fall of 2004, she was diagnosed with breast cancer. Coming fast on the heels of the highly publicized death of Brett's father, Irvin, and the unexpected loss of her younger brother, Casey, Deanna's diagnosis made her a reluctant celebrity virtually overnight.

Four years later and cancer-free, Deanna is one of breast cancer's leading activists. As the founder of the Deanna Favre HOPE Foundation, she now travels the country to raise funds and speak about the importance of early diagnosis. Deanna, Brett, and their daughters, Brittany and Breleigh, live in Hattiesburg, Mississippi.

Angela Hunt is the best-selling author of more than one hundred books, including *The Tale of Three Trees, The Note,* and *Magdalene.* She and her husband make their home in Florida.

Photograph of pink ribbon copyright © by Gary Woodard/iStockphoto. All rights reserved.

Front cover: Photo of Deanna Favre copyright © 2007 by Kaptions by Kristi. All rights reserved.

Back cover: Photo of Favre family copyright © 2000 by Turba Photography. All rights reserved.

Photo insert, page 3: Photo of Deanna Favre and Brittany (age 2) copyright © 1991 by Joe Giaise Studio. All rights reserved.

Photo insert, pages 4-5: Favre wedding photos copyright © 1996 by Jim Biever. All rights reserved.

Photo insert, page 7: Photo of Favre family with Jazzy the dog copyright © 2000 by Turba Photography. All rights reserved.

Photo insert, page 9: Photo of Deanna and Brittany Favre copyright © 2006 by Kaptions by Kristi. All rights reserved.

Photo insert, page 13: Photo of Deanna and Breleigh Favre at home in Mississippi copyright © 2004 by Kaptions by Kristi. All rights reserved.

Photo insert, page 14: Photo of Brett Favre copyright © 2006 by Mark A. Wallenfang. All rights reserved.

Photo insert, page 15: Photos of Brett and Deanna Favre copyright © 2003 by Mark A. Wallenfang. All rights reserved.

do it yourself
MONTHLY BREAST SELF-EXAM

STEP 1 • IN THE SHOWER

STEP 1

Place your right arm behind your head. With your left hand, examine your right breast. Using the pads of your three middle fingers, feel over the breast for lumps, thickness, or knots. Now place your left arm behind your head and use your right hand to examine your left breast. Do this the same day each month.

STEP 2 • IN FRONT OF MIRROR

STEP 2

While standing in each of the following three positions, look carefully for size, shape, and contour changes in each breast; or puckering, dimpling, or changes in skin texture: 1) arms at your sides, 2) arms above your head, and 3) hands firmly pressed on hips. Bow slightly forward while pulling shoulders forward.

Squeeze both nipples and look for a discharge.

STEP 3 • LYING DOWN

STEP 3

Lie down and place a pillow or towel under your right shoulder. Place your right hand behind your head. Examine your right breast with your left hand. Repeat the process for the opposite side.

3 METHODS FOR YOUR SELF-EXAM

Using your three middle finger pads, press firmly in small circles starting at the outermost top edge of your breast and spiral in toward the nipple (Fig. 1).

In addition to the spiral method you can also choose the vertical, up-and-down method (Fig. 2), or the wedge method (Fig. 3). Whichever method you choose, make sure to press firmly to feel all tissue, and do it the same way every time.

Be sure to check your underarm area, as this is also breast tissue. Rest your arm on a firm surface and use the same circular motion.

CALL YOUR DOCTOR IMMEDIATELY IF ANY CHANGES OR SYMPTOMS ARE NOTICED.

Periodic examinations by a qualified doctor are necessary. This is not a substitute.